NYLXS Journal

Volume 6 March 2015

Table of Content

ISBN 978-1-312-99551-2

Editorial Team: Micheal Richardson, Ruben Safir, with help contributions from Rick Moen

Contact Information: http://www.nylxs.com/

Copyright 2015 NYLXS and Authors licensed under the GNU Free Documentation License

Version 1.3, 3 November 2008 Referenced: https://www.gnu.org/copyleft/fdl.html

Special Adviser: Richard M Stallman

Special Thanks to Long Island University and Dr Samir Iabbassen for providing the learning experience that produced so many of these works.

NYLXS: We are Doers

Since November of 2000, NYLXS has been a leading Free Software Educational foundation in New York State with global outreach. NYLXS is all about its members and the volunteer and collaborative spirit that is at the core of Free Software. As we now enter our 15th year of existence, and now more than ever, the NYLXS credo of "We Are Do'ers" rings truer then ever before. In a digital environment where people and their personal lives are the product more than the consumer, protecting the individual in a digital civil society is getting harder and harder. We are being tracked, spied on, analyzed, and manipulated to an unprecedented degree, and this is all happening through your digital devices. As bad as it is, it looks like it will get worse. The only tool we have to fight back and keep out individuality is through Free Software and Free Software Education.

Only by putting free software in your hand, and gaining education can you form a free association that is resistant to exploitation, and impoverishment. Years ago, NYLXS talked about a future where we are all sharecroppers to our cultural heritage. We are now very close to the edge of that being a reality. We rush to put out personal papers on the "Cloud" when all along we have had the power to share and protect our papers within our grasps. It is not rocket science to have your own mail server, and your own webserver. In fact, most GNU/Linux distributions can do this out of the box with minimal education. So NYLXS fights to give you back your personal space. We teach, write, promote, and support free software for the public. We have classes, videos, radio shows, demonstations, tech meetings and programs to give anyone who wants it a head start. We close the digital divide, not but giving you an expensive tablet with some free music. We give you unlocked systems that you can shape to your individual needs, and then we show you how to do it. Join NYLXS and be a Do'er

~~~

Ruben Safir

02-2015

The New Dot Com Boom:

http://readwrite.com/2014/12/30/learning-to-code-2014-tech-education

It will tell you that young people today have more chances to code and learn to code than ever before.

I was in San Francisco for a Pharmacy Conference about a year ago when I noticed a new IT bubble in full gear. Oh, we've seen this before. The Saint Francis Hotel was packed with young hotties in their Mercedes-Benz, flush with a new generation of angle capital. Now, almost overnight, 8 month wonder programs are springing up all around NYC and the bubble has reached the east coast, full throttle. It all is so dizzying that it makes me look up to see if the twin towers are still standing. Alas, they are not and these young kids really think they have reinvented the wheel. I'm reading an article that tells me that people interested in IT today have more venues than ever to learn from. Is this true?

No, it is ignorance and inexperience being passed off as Jounralism by kids who may have never actually picked up a real news paper in their lives. This is not a generation of innovation. This is a generation that is so entraped they can't even see how deeply absorbed by marketing that they have become. After this last recession, BLINK was all the rage where Malcolm Gladwell had to teach us that it takes a few thousand hours to master any skill, and god knows that programming and running computer systems is a huge skill.

Well we have to go through this again? It looks like it.

It is unfortunate that one "reporter" can conclude that the opportunities to learn computer literacy and sciences has increased over the last few years. The opportunity has been available broadly and freely for decades now. In fact, the programs that you underline here, which are company produced, purchased and controlled platforms, are not helping anyone to better understand coding or Comp Sci principles. They are likely doing the opposite, obfuscating programming principles and narrowing coding options. The real opening for young people to learn to program began with and continues to be the GNU Free Software program.

GNU and Linux is the largest repository of freely available IT knowledge and educational material ever prodcued by man. It is the backbone of computer education and has opened the door for individuals to learn since its inception. From its early adoption and on until today, it has not only empowered the general population through information access, it has spurred communities, and has even raised the standards of living for 3rd world nations by giving them a leg up in the high tech field through sharing. Free Software, documentation and local community are the triumphant of computer science education for the empowered.

Today, however, there are fewer locally organized groups to support learning and hacking, and things are getting worse. The first thing people need to do in order to get better educated is put down your smart phone. Construction of an "app" in three days does not constitute any measure of technological knowledge. It actually means someone has been duped and is now a proudly dependent on very limited commercial toolkit. Real IT education requires much more work. It is the Real Deal. Real Math. Real Science. The Linux kernel, which was launched by a 21 year old programmer from Europe, contains as of 2013, with the 3.10 release 15,803,499 lines of code. Yeah that didn't happen in 3 days or ever a week. It didn't happen with the help of Apple or Microsoft or Sun or Unisys. In fact, it was the reverse. These companies, maybe all companies, now rely on the infrastructure of GNU and Free Software, in order to churn out profits, often just repackaging old ideas to a new clientel on a new platform.

While one can learn to be a productive coder with TUTELAGE, in a few years of hard work and study. You can't dispense with the tutelage, and you can't dispense with the practice and the work and you can not dispense with a community. This is where your local user groups step in and provide support. They also provide you with a measuring stick to judge your own capabilities. This can not happen surrounding yourself with peers and working with companies that want to exploit youthful enthusiasm. Unfortunately, user groups are all but dieing as their membership grow older with and gain private responsibilities. It doesn't help that you can't get the kids to dig their heads out of their smart phones.

As an example, a recent presentation at a local University for a computer group included "programming" flappy bird through object C. in one hour or less. They showed how to add some basic function code to an existing code base, and to press a button and compile it, and then flappy bird flaps. That was it, they learned Object C?

That's what they were told, if not outright, then as an implied message. They were awash in a glow of accomplishment. No. They didn't learn a damn thing but they got an excellent pitch to join a private coding school with "ties to start up entrepreneurial investors". The real documentation to learn ObjectC, however, IS available for free on line and has a diverse community of developers and users, supported by the GNU project. There is that word again, COMMUNITY and GNU. This is the

real Object C. In order to learn it, one starts with gnustep
http://www.gnustep.org/developers/documentation.html Here is the core manual with 148
pages, i think, or documentation of the objectC and gnustep core.
http://www.gnustep.org/resources/documentation/Developer/Base/ProgrammingManual/manual_toc.html

This is the base API http://www.gnustep.org/developers/documentation.html#objc

With the development of "apps", there
is a lot of renewed interest in ObjectC and GNUstep. But there is no
shortcuts to deep knowledge. Trust me, this current gold rush for IT
coders is not going to last long. There will be a crash, just like there
was after the dotcom boom and a dotcom crash.

If you expect to remain working in IT for 40 years, you are actually
going to have to learn something. You are going to need a good
background in C, C++, program design, Operating Systems, Systems
Security, Assembler, Architecture, and essential related math skills. A
background in LISP, Lamda Calculus, and relational theory can't hurt either.

The threat to your education is the very companies that want to exploit
young people today. They are trying to close off the access to tools and
documentation, ONCE AGAIN. Before the GNU project and Linux took root,
you have no idea how hard it was to get tools, education for comp sci,
and working software. ObjectC, for example,is threatened to be partially
closed by future apple development by skirting GNU copyright protections
for privatized development using the CLANG compiler, instead of GCC.
Instead of having it's development protected by the GPL, it will be
allocated according to the desires of Apple. Apple is not your friend.

Likewise, Oracle has moved the JAVA RTE to it's private sphere. These
"people" want to ensnare everyone. Will this generation coming be smart
enough to identify the threat to their own growth, empowerment and
education. Do you have a Richard Stallman among you. I don't think so.
Get your head out of the clouds, get your behind to a computer club and
be prepared to work. To me it looks bleak. too much candy crush, not
enough hard work and understanding.

**Ruben Safir is an MS in Comp
Sci Candidate at LIU Brooklyn
and Founder of NYLXS in 2000.
An accompished coder and
observer of the digital world,
he has been published and
contributes to the Brooklyn
community on a regular basis.
He is best contacted at
ruben@mrbrklyn.com**

The PCI Express Bus

Introduction

As an introduction to PCI Express bus, we will start talking about the theoretical and general shared bus structure in the PC style computer. We will follow this with a discussion of bus communication protocols. After that we will be ready to understand exactly how bus arbitration works. And Finally we will be focused on Peripheral Component Interconnect expresses (PCIe) device and its routing capability ties.

Shared bus structure

Bus technology connects components of computer system and is used to transport data between them. Aside from actual data, buses not only provides signaling information to ensure that data has reached its destination, but also provides for signaling flow control of data to ensure that the devices are ready to send or accept data when necessary. Flow control also defines at which speed two devices will communicate with each other. The bus consists of components that are connected by wires, and which usually appear as tracks on a Printed Circuit Board (PCB).

There are four types of buses: address, power, control, and data. Buses consists of a number of parallel lines that are connected between the memory, CPU and I/O devices. The information on the address bus allows memory and I/O devices to be accessed (by their address). The data bus , also, consists of parallel lines. Data buses are used to send data and instructions. Control buses are a collection of lines designated for tasks such as request, write, read and reset. Power buses provide basic power to devices.

Speed of data transfer

Buses can be built in two modes: serial and parallel. In serial mode, data is transferred one bit at a time. In parallel mode data is sent multiple bits at a time. For example, if an 8-bit character is sent using serial mode, it will be sent bit by bit. But in parallel mode, 8 bits are sent simultaneously at a time through 8 separate wires. Parallel mode has some some problems that must be overcome. When an electric current is sent through the wire, it is creating the electromagnetic field that may influence the adjacent electric currents. In this case, the receiving device may get incorrect data. This is called Electromagnetic Interference (EMI). Wires on a motherboard, being imperfect, are not always the same size. When a bit is sent through the shorter wire, it will get to destination faster than other bits sent in a parallel set. This results the receiving device having to wait until all bits are arrive, which causes issue called propagation delay.

Data on a bus can be sent at burst or sustained rate. The burst rate is a maximum rate at which data can be sent over a bus. The sustained rate is a rate at which data can be sent over a bus in a constant manner. To understand these rates, let's look at the analogy of the sprint runner and the long distance runner. A sprint runner can run with a very high speed in a short time, but he cannot maintain his speed. Long distance runner maintains his constant speed to reach a specific location. This example reflects the key difference between these two rates and this concept applies to buses. The sustained rate is better metric, because it reflects the typical transmission speed.

Shared bus protocols

A protocol is a set of rules agreed upon by buses as to how information is to be sent over the bus. One of the main functions of bus protocol is Flow control. Suppose that two computers are communicating with each other for uploading or downloading data. At some point, one of the computers will need to store the received information on a disk. But what happens if computer is receiving data while writing file on a disk? That's where flow control plays its role.

Flow control allows the receiving device to regulate the flow of data sent by the sending device. Some protocols allow two communicating devices to agree upon the size of block to be sent to each other. A block is a portion of the data which the protocol defines. The data is divided into packages of a specific size, a defined block. These blocks are usually either of 128, 256, 512, 1024, or 2048 Kbytes in size. Mechanisms exists to ensure that the data received by the receiving device is correct. The sending device performs calculations on the block that it is will send. This might be 1 to 2 bytes called a Block Check Character (BCC). When the receiving device receives the block, it also starts to calculate BCC of the data in the block. The receiving device compares the value of BCC, both which it computed and that which it received. If they are equal, then the receiving device informs the sending device that everything is alright. If BCC values are not equal, the receiving device asks the sending device to resend the block. The sending device transmits only one block at a time.

Bus protocols can be open or proprietary. In order to connect a device to a bus, for example, the PCI bus (which we will cover later), the device, and the software which runs it, must be implemented with PCI bus protocol to the letter. The main reason of having different standards are business strategies. Usually the most successful bus protocols are open standards, which PCI is. Manufacturers are not obliged to pay money to the developer for implementing PCI into the devices that they are creating. This allows different manufacturers to compete with other manufacturers while ensuring the buyer that their product will be working on every computer that includes a PCI bus.

Buses can operate using synchronous, asynchronous or semi-synchronous communication protocols. A device that starts a read or write operation is called the master device. A device that the master device communicates with is called a slave device. If, for example, CPU requests data from memory (Read operation), then the CPU is a master device and the memory is a slave device.

Asynchronous bus devices are not supposed to send or receive data at the fixed clock rate. Additional handshake lines will be needed to guarantee that information is sent or received. This mode can achieve the maximum throughput between devices and allows the slow and fast devices to communicate with each other. Asynchronous protocols use two control signals: MSYNC (Master sync signal) – which is sent by a master device, indicating that it is ready and SSYNC (Slave sync signal) – which is sent by slave device, indicating that it is ready.

Let's look at the steps of the CPU (master) reading data from memory (slave) using asynchronous protocol:

1) CPU sends address information and asserts MREQ and READ. Address information indicates where exactly the required information is located in memory. Asserting MREQ (memory request) and READ indicates that CPU requests information from memory;

2) CPU asserts MSYNC. The most important thing to remember here is that MSYNC must be asserted after asserting the triplet of MREQ, READ and sending address information. The MSYNC signal states that the currently asserted MREQ, READ and sent address information are correct;

3) CPU waits for the SSYNC signal response from memory;

4) After receiving SSYNC signal from memory, CPU copies the received data into MBR (Memory Buffer Register);

5) CPU removes MSYNC request. Again, MSYNC must be removed before removing MREQ and READ requests due to the same reasons mentioned before;

6) CPU removes address information, MREQ and READ requests.

Figure 1 illustrates the example of asynchronous protocol:

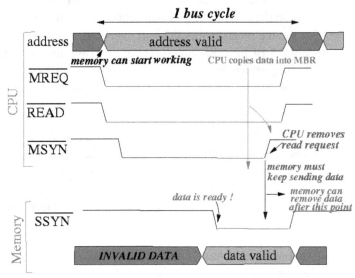

Synchronous bus devices communicate with each other at a fixed clock rate. This clock dictates when exactly the data will arrive in a certain time range. If a device hasn't received data in certain clock time, data is lost. Synchronous transfer occurs in register-to-register transfer within the CPU. Let's look at the steps of the CPU reading data from memory using synchronous protocol:

1) At rise of a clock, CPU sends address information;

2) At fall of a clock, CPU asserts MREQ and READ to request data from memory;

3) At fall of next clock, memory is ready to send the data to the CPU. After copying data into MBR, CPU removes address information, MREQ and READ.

Figure 2 illustrates the example of synchronous protocol

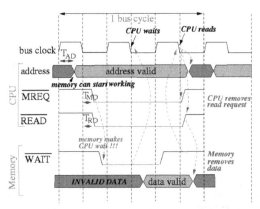

The WAIT signal informs CPU that it should wait before the data from memory is ready. It is expected that some event is going at occur at a rise/fall of the bus clock, but these events do not occur immediately due to physics: some time is required for clock signal to travel from bus to CPU. In the Figure 2, these delays are marked as:

T_{AD} – Delay between rise of a clock and sending address information;

T_{MD} – Delay between fall of a clock and asserting MREQ;

T_{RD} – Delay between fall of a clock and asserting READ.

Semi-synchronous mode combines benefits of synchronous and asynchronous modes. It has the speed of synchronous bus and allows different slow and fast devices to communicate with each other. In semi-synchronous mode the communication between master and slave is still regulated by fixed clock rate, but if a slave is not be able to provide data to the master in the required time, it will be allowed to send data during several clock cycles. Example of semi-synchronous communication is between CPU and Main memory.

There are two types of buses: Dedicated and Multiplexed. Dedicated bus has only one function (address or data). Multiplexed buses consist of lines that act like an address bus or data bus in a shared period of time. This means that in one period the bus transfers address information and in another period bus transfers data information. This type of a bus was used in earlier microcomputers and is cheaper than dedicated bus, but it is slower. Modern high performance computers use dedicated buses.

A bus cannot be used by several devices at the same time. This is because of the electrical properties of the devices (it can cause damage). A solution for this is arbitration: devices get permission before sending information. Bus arbitration and bus utilization always happen at the same time. While the bus is currently being used, other devices which are competing for bus access elect which one of them is going to use the bus next time.

There are two types of arbitration: Centralized and Distributed. In centralized arbitration there is only one master which gives permission to slave devices. Let's look at centralized arbiter of PCI bus:

PCI's centralized arbitration depends on the priority of slave devices. In this case, a device with the highest number has highest priority. By looking at the Table 1, you may notice that PCI Dev 2 always has the highest priority comparing to other devices. If the value of ReqX (X=0,1,2) equals to 1, then PCI Dev X (X=0,1,2) sends request for the bus usage. Otherwise, if ReqX equals to 0, then the device is idle. If GrantX equals to 1, PCI Arbiter grants PCI Dev X permission for using the bus.

In distributed arbitration, there is no central controller. In this case, control logic is on every device. Figure 5 illustrates this scenario

Bus Types and Standards

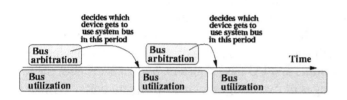

PCI (Peripheral Component Interconnect) is a 32 bit synchronous bus with multiplexed address and data lines that can run at up to 33Mhz clock rate. This bus transfers data in parallel mode.

AGP (Accelerated Graphics Port) is a bus for video cards which also transfer data in parallel mode. AGP was a successor to the PCI bus. Over the time, video adapters have evolved and became bandwith-hungry. PCI's shared bus architecture constrained the devices from operating at full speed. AGP is using point-to-point architecture which allows direct communication with CPU without sharing a bus. It also uses dedicated data and address lines so the entire packet does not need to be read to get the address. Graphic adapters use a separate 8-bit "SideBand address" bus to send AGP request and command information while using 32 data/address lines to send data at the same time. The other advantage is that for loading textures, AGP graphic card can directly read textures from the main memory whereas PCI graphic card must first copy these textures from main memory to card's video memory and then read them.

Req2	Req1	Req0	Grant 2	Grant 1	Grant 0
0	0	0	0	0	0
0	0	1	0	0	1
0	1	0	0	1	0
0	1	1	0	1	0
1	0	0	1	0	0
1	0	1	1	0	0
1	1	0	1	0	0
1	1	1	1	0	0

PCIe (Peripheral Component Interconnect express)

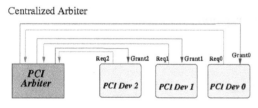

A better version of PCI bus was invented with the name of PCIe (Peripheral Component Interconnect express). Currently this is the most popular bus used in contemporary computer systems, which replaced the older PCI, PCI-X and AGP buses. PCIe transfers data in serial mode.

PCIe is implemented using the point-to-point topology. PCIe devices communicate with each other using a packet based communications protocol, which is similar to the TCP/IP protocols used in the computer networks. It is available in a variety of different physical configuration, such as x1, x4, x8, x16, x32 and it is upward and downward compatible. The PCIe x4 card can be fit into every single PCIe slot (x1, x4, x8, x16), but if PCIe card's configuration is lower than the PCIe slot's, it will have less bandwith. In case of x1 slot, PCIe x4 card's bandwith will be limited to PCIe x1 slot's bandwith. In case of x16 slot, PCIe x4 card's bandwith won't be limited, but it still won't be able to have more bandwith than its own architecture. PCIe is backward compatible with PCI, meaning that PCI software can still detect and work with PCIe, but it won't be able to use all features of PCIe.

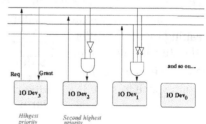

The available bandwith of PCIe card is not only dictated by the PCIe slot length. Version is another parameter that affects PCIe card's bandwith. There are four versions (generations) of PCIe.

As you can see by looking at the table 2, the available bandwith of PCIe card is almost doubled with each version. For example, the available bandwith of x16 card with PCIe version 1 equals to x4 card with PCIe version 3. If the PCIe card is going to be attached to the PCI slot with different version, then the available bandwith will be identified by the lowest version between card and slot. PCIe also includes features like Quality of Service (QoS), hot plug & hot swap support, advanced power management.

Memory read request from the CPU targeting specific Endpoint Though a PCIexp

The figure below graphically illustrates a memory read request from a CPU targeting a specific endpoint. The Root Complex, on behalf of a processor starts the non-posted memory read transaction by creating the MRd (Memory read request) packet. Amongst other information, this packet contains a requester ID (which is Root Complex in this case), targeted address, packet type and length of transfer (doublewords). The root complex sends this packet to the switch's upstream port (the port which points to the root complex). The switch can be logically represented as three PCI-to-PCI bridges connected to each other via internal bus as shown in the below, showing the case of the switch having five PCI-to-PCI bridges. Each bridge contains memory, address limits and I/O base registers. Switch A decodes the MRd packet and compares its values with base/limit addresses ranges of two bridges with downstream ports. When Switch A finds the right port, it forwards the packet to that port, such as Switch B. Switch B performs a similarly routine to find the right port.

When the endpoint receives the MRd, it will accept this packet and create completion packet (CpID). CpID also includes requester ID (bus#, device#, function #) in its overhead (which was copied from MRd) so that this packet could be routed back to the Root Complex. When CpID arrives to switch B, the switch is routing the packet based on the bus number of requester ID. When CpID is received by switch A from switch B, it routes the packet similarly. Finally, when Root Complex receives the CpID, it compares the value of receiver ID field in CpID's overhead with its own ID. If ID is correct and CpID has no errors, then it is forwarded to processor.

PCIe is a layered protocol. It consists of software, physical, data link and transaction layers.

Transaction layer

The transaction layer packet (TLP) originates at TLP. Transaction layer has virtual channels buffers (VC) that hold TLP arrived from software or link layers. One of the main functions of Transaction layer is Flow control, which ensures that the transmitter will not overload these buffers with TLPs . Flow control is based on credit scheme, meaning that transmitter will only send TLP when the receiver's buffer has enough space to store it.

	Version 1	Version 2	Version 3	Version 4
Bandwith in each direction, per lane	250 MB/s	500 MB/s	984.6 MB/s	1969.2 MB/s

Data link layer

The data link layer ensures the data integrity of the packets that are sent or received by two adjacent devices. It also checks the LCRC values and the sequencing of the packets. The data link layer generates three important types of data link layer packets (DLLP) – acknowledge or no acknowledge (ACK/NAK), flow control (FCx) and power management (PMx). When the transmitter sends the TLP packet, it must be sure that this packet reached the receiver without any problems. Before transmitting any packet, the transmitter copies the TLP into a special buffer named the replay buffer (or Retry Buffer). If the packet is lost during transmission or reached the receiver in "corrupted" state, the receiver must inform transmitter to resend the packet. ACK/NAK protocol is used to acknowledge the transmitter about

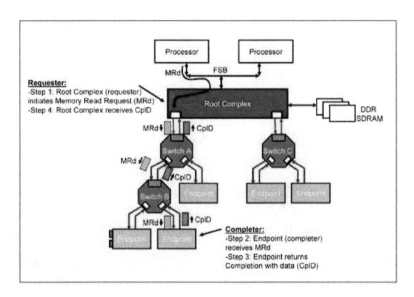

the packet arrival. If the packet arrived, then receiver sends ACK message to inform transmitter that everything is OK. After receiving ACK message, transmitter can remove TLP from the replay buffer. The receiver sends NAK when the TLP packet has a wrong CRC (LCRC) value. If transmitter has received NAK 4 times and replayed the TLP 3 times, then it logs error and retrains the link. If transmitter hasn't received any ACK messages or received NAK message, then transmitter must resend the TLP and all other packets that were sent after it. This method resolves the problem of DLLPs not being acknowledged. For example, the transmitter was acknowledged with ACK, but this DLLP has a bad CRC value. The transmitter will not acknowledge receiver about this problem and will resend the TLP packet again.

What if Replay Buffer gets overloaded because transmitter doesn't receive ACK from the receiver fast enough? Thankfully there is a time period in which the receiver must answer the transmitter about the received packet. This technique prevents the replay buffer from getting overloaded over a short period of time and helps calculate the appropriate size of a replay buffer. Sure it would be more convenient to have a replay buffer with a huge memory so there couldn't be any overload problems, but this will make the price of PCIe device very big, which is not an appealing thing for a buyer.

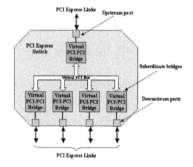

Physical Layer

Physical layer describes the electrical characteristics of PCIe. This layer generates ordered sets (PLP) which is used for linking management and is exchanged between the physical layers between transmitters and receivers. The transmission unit of physical layer is called a lane and consists of two pairs of wires, one of which is for transmitting and another one is for receiving data. PCIe devices communicate with each other in full-duplex mode, meaning that they can receive and send data at the same time. So why do we need two wires for each direction? This is because of the technique called Differential Signaling. To understand this technique, we should mention Single Ended Signaling that was used in PCI:

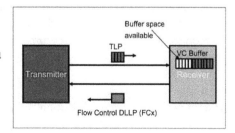

Figure 10 illustrates that in the case of Single Ended Signaling, there is only one wire used to send the signal and the receiver reads the signal as 1 if it is supplied with 5V. In the case of differential signaling, the second wire is used to send a "mirrored" signal (inverted polarity). The receiver identifies 0 or 1 by finding the difference between the volt of blue and black line. If the difference between the volt of blue and black line is higher than a certain value, then it is signified as a 0; if the difference is lower, the result is 1. The Differential Signaling technique is better because it is faster to adjust the voltage if we need different value (from 0 to 1 or from 1 to 0). The other reason is that it has more immunity to noise. The illustration below illustrates this condition. When noise occurs, both of the wires are going to get affected by it. So no matter if the noise occurred in the bus or not, the volt difference between the two signals is always going to be the same.

PCIe addressing and routing

When a device receives a packet at an ingress port, it first checks this packet for errors and then decides whether: 1) Accept the packet; 2) Forward the packet to other egress port (if it has them); 3) Reject the packet. Receivers check the incoming type of packet to determine whether to forward this packet. If the packet type is DLLP or PLP, it is not going to be forwarded through other ports of the receiver. These packets do not contain any routing information in their headers and solely intended for link management between two adjacent devices. TLP is the only type of packet that is going to be forwarded and it contains routing information in its header. Devices that contain multiple ports (e.g. Switch, Root Complex) are intended to perform routing function on the packets. Endpoints are limited in their routing capabilities, which means that they can only accept or reject TLPs. Before devices can accept, forward or reject data, they must be configured to do so. Using plug and play, they first must be discovered. Then they are assigned with memory and I/O address resources and programmed with routing.

PCIe TLP routing basics

TLP uses four address spaces: memory, I/O, configuration and messaging. Memory address space used to address system memory or I/O memory. I/O address space is used to address legacy PCI devices. Configuration address space is used to address register of a specific I/O device. Message address space is used for control signals.

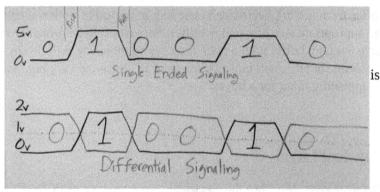

is

Split transaction technique is used when transmitter sends non-posted request packet. It awaits for a completion packet from the receiver. This means that two separate transactions will be used to send the request and completion packets at different times. The receiver will send a completion packet only after it finds the requested data and is ready to send packets. This is much better than old technique used by PCI bus, which required two devices to seize the whole bus for transaction. This resulted in big delays because of busyness of the bus and packet retransmission in case of an error.

TLPs can be routed using address routing, ID routing and implicit routing. Memory and I/O transactions are routed using address routing. ID routing is used to find the logical location of registers within PCI compatible bus (IDs consist of the bus, device and function numbers). Implicit routing is used when a packet needs to reach a device which is known and has fixed position (e.g. Root Complex).

TLP consists of 3 or 4 DoubleWords which are 12 and 16 bytes long respectively. Type fields identify which routing is going to be used with this packet. This chart illustrates the header structure of TLP:

When TLP is received at the ingress port, checks are made first by the physical and data links layers for errors. If there are no errors the transaction layer starts to be examined. The first double word is looked at in the TLP.

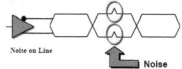

Then it will check if the TLP arrived its intended recipient or not. If yes, it will be accepted. If it is not the intended recipient, and it is a device with multiple ports, then the TLP will be forwarded to the respective egress port. If this is not intended recipient and is not the device which is located on the way to the recipient, then the packet will be rejected.

Address Routing

Address routing is used to route TLPs destined to or originating from memory, direct mapped I/O and I/O devices. The address range In TLP's overhead can be 32 bits using 3DW or 64 bits using 4DW. Legacy I/O devices cannot be addressed with 64-bit addresses.

When an endpoint receives TLP indicating the address routing in the Type field, it simply compares the address in TLP's overhead with its BAR (Base Address Register). BAR is a register which keeps the device's address. If two compared addresses are equal, then endpoint accepts the packet. Otherwise it is going to reject it.

When a switch receives TLP indicating the address routing in the type field, it first resolves if the switch is the intended recipient. If not, it compares the address in TLP's overhead with Base and Limit registers of each PCI-to-PCI bridge (with egress ports). Base and Limit registers identify the range of addresses located through the specific port. For example, If Base register has value 100 and limit register has value 200, it means that devices with addresses 100-200 are located through this port. Upstream TLPs are always routed through the upstream port if they do not match the base and limit registers and are not intended for this switch.

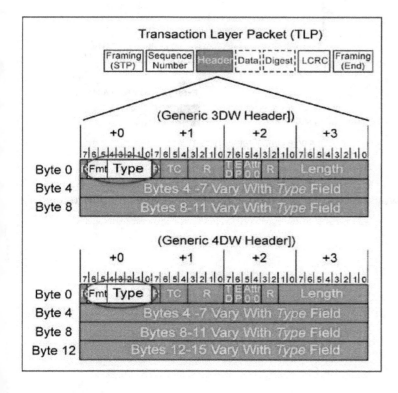

ID Routing

In ID routing the devices route the TLPs using ID (bus + device + function numbers) numbers. This addressing was used in PCI and PCI-X topology. ID routing is also used with completion and message packets. There are limits on bus, device and function numbers. PCIe topology can consist of maximum 256 buses, 32 devices on each bus and 8 functions on each device.

When an endpoint receives TLP with type indicating ID routing, it compares its bus, device and function numbers with ID number of TLP's overhead. If comparing values are equal, then the device accepts the TLP. Otherwise, it will reject the packet.

Similar to endpoints, switches first compares its bus, device and function numbers with ID number of TLP's overhead. If comparing values are equal, then the device accepts the TLP. If not, the switch starts to compare the bus number value of TLP's overhead with range of secondary-subordinate registers of each PCI-to-PCI bridges. Secondary register contains the bus number that is directly attached to the downstream port. Subordinate register contains farthest & largest bus number of downstream device located through the downstream port. Upstream TLPs are always routed through the upstream port if they do not match the range of secondary-subordinate registers and are not intended for this switch.

Implicit Routing

Implicit routing is used when there is a need to inform the device with known and fixed position (such as Root Complex) about power, error, interrupt management problems. Implicit routing can be used only with message TLPs.

Message TLPs can also be routed using address or ID routing. First 3 bits of the type field (which is 5 bits long) identify the type of routing and where this packet should be sent. Table 3 shows all cases. The last 2 bits of the type field identify whether or not this is a message TLP. Message TLP can also be sent as a broadcast packets from root complex.

When an endpoint receives the message TLP, it will check the first 3 bits to figure out the routing type and if this packet is appropriate for it. For example, it won't receive the message that was intended for Root Complex.

Similar to the endpoint, a switch will check the first 3 bits to figure out the routing type and if this packet is appropriate for it. For example, if a switch receives broadcast message TLP on its uplink port, it will spread this packet through all downstream ports. It won't accept broadcast message that will be received through the

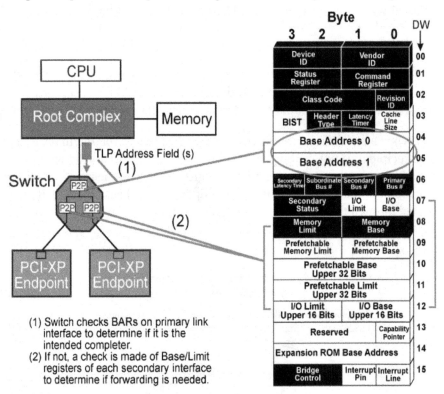

(1) Switch checks BARs on primary link interface to determine if it is the intended completer.
(2) If not, a check is made of Base/Limit registers of each secondary interface to determine if forwarding is needed.

Note: To conserve space, a single configuration Type 1 header is shown. Of course each switch port has its own Type 1 configuration header.

downstream port. Another example is that the switch won't accept the implicitly indicated message pointing to the Root Complex if this message was received at uplink port.

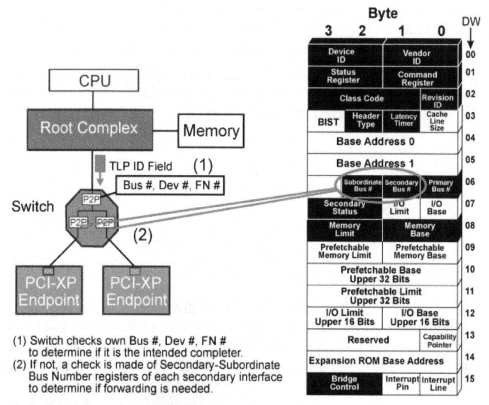

Byte

3	2	1	0	DW
Device ID		Vendor ID		00
Status Register		Command Register		01
Class Code			Revision ID	02
BIST	Header Type	Latency Timer	Cache Line Size	03
Base Address 0				04
Base Address 1				05
Subordinate Bus #	Secondary Bus #		Primary Bus #	06
Secondary Status		I/O Limit	I/O Base	07
Memory Limit		Memory Base		08
Prefetchable Memory Limit		Prefetchable Memory Base		09
Prefetchable Base Upper 32 Bits				10
Prefetchable Limit Upper 32 Bits				11
I/O Limit Upper 16 Bits		I/O Base Upper 16 Bits		12
Reserved			Capability Pointer	13
Expansion ROM Base Address				14
Bridge Control		Interrupt Pin	Interrupt Line	15

(1) Switch checks own Bus #, Dev #, FN # to determine if it is the intended completer.
(2) If not, a check is made of Secondary-Subordinate Bus Number registers of each secondary interface to determine if forwarding is needed.

Note: For space, a single configuration Type 1 header is shown. Each link interface has its own.

References:

http://www.lintech.org/comp-per/01buses__ver2_.pdf

http://en.wikipedia.org/wiki/System_bus

http://www.mathcs.emory.edu/~cheung/Courses/355/Syllabus/5-bus/asynch-bus.html

http://en.wikipedia.org/wiki/PCI_Express

http://www.hardwaresecrets.com/article/Everything-You-Need-to-Know-About-the-PCI-Express/190/2 - Gabriel Torres, 2012

http://www.mindshare.com/files/resources/mindshare_pcie_replay_buffer_sizing.pdf - Joe Winkles, 2003

http://www.plxtech.com/files/pdf/technical/expresslane/TechnologyBrief_PCIExpress_Q4-2003.pdf

http://pciexpress-datalinklayer.blogspot.com/ - 2008

http://www.icverification.com/BusProtocols/PCIE.php

Kamran Mirzoyev is a 2nd year Masters Degree Candidate from Long Island

University Brooklyn. Originally from Baku Azerbaijan, he has a BS Degree in Computer Sciences and a strong interest in Hardware and the History of Computer Sciences.

CyanogenMod: More Android than Android

A look at the most popular aftermarket firmware based on the Android operating system

Written by Robert Menes – 2/13/15

INTRODUCTION

Most F/OSS advocates should be celebrating something: Had Android not arrived on the scene in September 2008, the mobile phone market would be a very different beast right now at the time of this writing. At the time, Microsoft and Apple held what could be considered a duopoly on the smartphone market with Windows Mobile and iOS, respectively. Blackberries were still hot shit, and Linux was starting to make some headway into the market with Nokia's Maemo-based Internet Tablet devices. Google's announcement of a mobile OS based on the Linux kernel surprised a lot of people and had its share of naysayers in the beginning, but Android managed to climb from being the scrappy little underdog to the proverbial king of the mobile OS ecosystem, with, as of this writing, 79% of all mobile devices (phones, tablets, video streaming devices) running Android in some form or another.

Soon after Android was released, the community that began to grow around it had found a root exploit that allowed one to gain root user rights to the system via the bash shell, and telnet into the system itself. With that, intrepid hackers were able to alter, rewrite, and back up the entire system. Backing up the system allowed hackers to modify and change portions of the OS, and then flash the modified OS back onto their devices. One of these developers, JesusFreke, developed a rather popular modified Android for HTC Dream users, but it was a fork of JesusFreke's modified system, CyanogenMod, which featured further enhancements and changes, and it rapidly became much more popular and known.

So, what is CyanogenMod? Simply put, CyanogenMod could be called a modded Android. But to stop there would be doing it wrong. CyanogenMod is everything Android is, and then some. Originally running on only the HTC Dream, the first Android phone on the market, support rapidly spread to new devices as they came onto the market. The HTC Magic, the successor to the Dream, gained support quickly due to similar hardware. As the Android market grew, more phones continued to gain support, though this also depended on OEMs playing nice and following the software licenses of Android (the Linux kernel is GPLv2; the rest of the OS is Apache 2.0) and release the necessary source code for the modifications to the kernel. Today, CyanogenMod has been ported to (officially) 257 different devices; a great deal many more unofficial ports exist on community sites, such as XDA Developers, and anyone could start a port of their own by downloading the CyanogenMod source from GitHub and adding needed information about the device and any additional hardware blobs needed.

CUSTOMIZATION & FEATURES

Compared to the stock experience from the Android Open Source Project (herein "AOSP"), CyanogenMod's draw was, and still is, many additional features that either Google or cellular carries had excluded from the Android builds of many devices. USB tethering and Wifi hotspot support are among the more popular features that many carriers do not offer due to data usage issues (in their words). But we're just scraping the surface if we stop there.

CyanogenMod is completely user customizable; you are not in any way, shape, or form locked onto Google's ecosystem of services. While an optional install for new CM users, the Google services are not mandatory, and you can use alternative markets and repositories for installing and managing apps, such as AppBrain or F-Droid. Sideloading apps is also possible; CM doesn't deny users their freedom to use and install apps how they wish.

This customization stretches to the user interface as well. CyanogenMod uses its own launcher, Trebuchet, by default, but you're not limited to using it alone. With a plethora of alternative launchers for Android (like a personal favorite, Nova Launcher), plus themes and icon packs created by users and designers, CM's looks and UI can be put together in the way you feel comfortable.

Under the hood, CyanogenMod sports a plethora of customizable functions and features. One of these, Privacy Guard, gives a tremendous amount of control over app permissions. You can either set Privacy Guard to broadly deny permissions to an app, or finely adjust the controls so you can set certain permissions off. Don't want an app to access your contacts? Block its access to your contacts with a switch. Don't want Facebook to use your camera? Deny it access to both cameras. Instagram sending information behind your back? Don't allow it to send data without your consent. Your privacy in your hands, not in the hands of a manufacturer or a carrier.

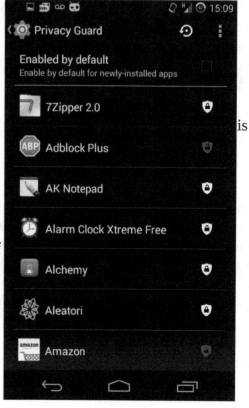

Additionally, CyanogenMod features SMS encryption built in, using WhisperPush. WhisperPush is an integrated, system-wide secure messaging system based on TextSecure, an open-source, cross-platform client that encrypts SMS messages both locally on the device, and when sending to other TextSecure users. In other words, if you and your friends are using CyanogenMod, and therefore WhisperPush, all of your text messages are fully encrypted and private, keeping your conversations safe from prying eyes and third parties. Additionally, the entire phone itself can be fully encrypted, further protecting all of the data you keep on your device from unwanted outsiders.

As rooting an Android is a popular undertaking for many users, CyanogenMod is naturally easy to gain root access in. Although for security purposes root access is disabled by default, it is easy to enable via an app such as SuperSU or the original Superuser app.

INSTALLATION

So this all sounds really awesome, right? You're going to want to know if installation of CyanogenMod is easy to accomplish. And the answer is that, for the most part, CyanogenMod is easy to install on many devices. Some devices, like the Nexus line from Google, are extremely easy to install CyanogenMod on. For the Nexus devices, all that is required is a CM build, an alternative recovery system like TeamWin or ClockworkMod Recovery, and two software tools from the Android development kit: adb and fastboot. You'll also need basic knowledge of using the terminal of the OS of your choice (Windows, OS X, or Linux).

The process is simple: enable USB debugging on your device, then from the bootloader, simply enter '`adb reboot bootloader`' and allow the device to reboot. From there, verify that fastboot can see the device by typing '`fastboot devices`', and if it's seen, simply enter '`fastboot oem unlock`', agree to unlocking the bootloader, and presto; your phone is officially unlocked! Note that unlocking the bootloader will erase anything on the phone, so be sure to either back up your phone first, or do these steps on a brand new, out-of-box device.

From there, flashing a new recovery is easily done with the command '`fastboot flash recovery your_recovery_image.img`'. Installation of CM itself is done through flashing via recovery. Simply back up the old OS, wipe, then flash CM, and reboot. Your phone should start up with CyanogenMod, and after a few minutes, you'll be asked if you want to create a CyanogenMod account, which will allow you to sync settings and services among phones. This step is completely optional; you are allowed to opt out if you wish.

While out of the box, CyanogenMod uses a majority of the AOSP apps by default, you can easily remove any apps you don't want and replace them with other apps as you choose. As mentioned earlier, you are not forced into using apps you don't want. CyanogenMod contains no bloatware from OEMs or carriers, and none of the default apps are "locked" to the system. It is nothing but a clean, fast, smooth experience; no added fillers.

FINAL THOUGHTS

CyanogenMod is everything that Android should be, and much more. Most people may be satisfied with their phones as they come from OEMs and carriers, but those who want a fast, simple Android experience without added garbage bogging down the works (seriously, who needs apps from carriers like Verizon or AT&T?), CyanogenMod delivers on that promise in spades. Plus, when most carriers and OEMs abandon older devices simply because a new device comes out, older devices can be given a new lease on life with CyanogenMod. For example, while Samsung may be hawking a new Galaxy S phone annually, not everyone can purchase one right away, and older Galaxy phones are stuck on older Android versions; Samsung doesn't believe these phones to be worth their time anymore. However, CyanogenMod, currently based on Android 4.4 "KitKat (currently their "stable" release) are available for all of the Galaxy S line, including the original Galaxy S.

All in all, CyanogenMod should be used by anyone who wants more out of their phone than just the OEM experience, or still has an older phone that deserves a better treatment than being left in the dust by carriers and OEMs. Install instructions for all supported devices are available via their wiki, and the community support built around the project is excellent and able to help with most any situation you may come across. CyanogenMod is a serious alternative to the stock AOSP experience and comes highly recommended.

LINKS:

CyanogenMod homepage: http://www.cyanogenmod.org/

Support Device listing: http://wiki.cyanogenmod.org/w/Devices

Source code: https://github.com/CyanogenMod

XDA Developers: http://www.xda-developers.com/

Robert Menes: NYLUG Hackers Club Leader: Blogger, writer, silly person at The Internet, Associate Entertainment and Media Correspondent at Maglomaniac and Community Volunteer at Drupal

UEFI – the New Booting Process for x86 systems

IBM/PC/Intel Based computers, like all other computing systems, need to boot when they are powered on. The computer's various parts and in and out devices need to be defined in order to allow access to resources. In order to facilitate booting, PC based systems have a variety of ROM like storage systems to read the program that begins the booting process.

When a computer starts, it has no knowledge of itself. It is a blank slate. All the information that the system needs to know about itself, in order to process user programs and to do useful tasks, requires an increasingly complex task of making resources available and known. In order to do this, systems are hard wired to look for the starting
instructions at fixed locations on the system. These locations are specific for different hardware types. For example on Intel x86 processors, memory location FFFF:0000 is always the first instruction that the CPU is begin executing with. Other systems have different locations, and even different addressing schemes.

Intel x86 based system include ROM based firmware called a BIOS. The BIOS (Basic Input/Ouptput System), has exacting specifications. Although they can vary, for a specific x86 type of architecture, they can only vary within the confines of the specification. A BIOS relies on the x86 architecture's 16-bit real mode which is a long was of saying that it works in the environment of a 16 bit CPU of the x86 type. Since all the intel chips have been backwardly compatible to this standard, up
until now, BIOS, and CMOS software that accesses the BIOS has been at the core of system start ups for intel based hardware for a generation.

Over time, there has been increasing demands on hardware booting. Even early in the history of the PC, there was a need to use PCs as thin clients and for network booting. This required that network cards, and networking protocols to be active prior to the booting and implementation of the operating system. There was the creation of the BOOTP and TFTP (trivial FTP) and a slowly a whole alphabet soup of acronyms have been introduced into the lingo of booting system.

In addition to this, more than one operating system are now installed on system, and hard drive capacities have grown further that the 16 BIOSaddressing scheme can read. Hard Drives have had master boot records, but over time, booting information has moved off the master boot record and onto various partitions. Additionally, modern Free Software and proprietary systems can run on a variety of hardware outside of the world of the x86 architecture.

Bios and CMOS can now also be flashed, to be updated and allow for more flexible configurations. Tablets, micro-tables(phones), and new laptop designs with touch screen are standard input devices have become population. All this has put pressure to redesign the booting system for commodity hardware.

"In the end, the BIOS is still here and still does what it has been doing for the last 25 years: making sure your operating system can boot. It was never designed for today's massive diversity of hardware. It's still stuck with 16-bit interfaces and software interrupts, interrupt routing and maximum precision timers, limited ROM execution space (1MB) and image size, a limited number of initializeable devices (which is critical in the server space), proprietary extensions, and missing modularity—just to name a few issues." [1]

This has been a blessing and a curse. Efforts to remove the BIOS functionality have always been targeted to take away the flexibility of run anything, clean and simple interface. IBM's MicroChannel architecture is but one an example. Intel finally took the bull by the horns with the introduction of the Itanium's IA64 architecture (along with HP) in 2003. This was a PC like server architecture that needed around some of the BIOS limitations. The created the EFI standards (adding more acronyms to the soup), and handed off its future to the industrial consortium called Unified Extensible Firmware Interface Forum which is an acronym for AMD, Insyde Software, American Megatrends, Inc.. Intel, Apple Inc, Lenovo, Dell, Microsoft, Hewlett Packard, Phoenix Technologies and IBM. There is a SINGLE non-profit engineering or standards group represented on UEFI forum. The result is some very useful specifications a washed in some game changing lock down mechanism designed to do what IBM could never accomplish with microchannel.

UEFI, in fact, is nearly an operating system sitting between your firmware and your operating system. "It not only offers driver support, interfaces, and services, but it also has a shell that allows users to execute applications on a command line interface." [1]

The generalized process of UEFI booting is as follows:

1- UEFI Firmware: Performs CPU and Chipset initialization and loadsdrivers

2- UEFI Boot Manager - Loads device drivers and the boot application

3- Loads the OS boot manager selected by the user

4- Loads the OS

5- Runs the OS Kernel

EFI (the Intel Child of UEFI) has tables and offers run level services to the operatings. This is similar to the runtime services that unix-like operating systems have had for decades. Boot Services includefile services, text and graphic user consoles, and the run services can offer access to Non-volatile random-access memory (NVRAM), date and time, etc. EFI drivers have specific communication protocols that all components can use. The EFI device driver environment s a virtualdrive, like what Java uses, called the EBC, which provides a CPU independent development target for UEFI module development.

Overall Boot Time line
Part 1:
Power On
Secure Boot
Pre EFI Initialization (PEI)
PIE Core
CPU Init
Chipset Init
Board Iniit
EFI Driver Dispatcher
Architecture Protocols
Driver Execution Environment
Device, Bus and Service Driver
Utilization of the EFI Driver Dispatcher

Boot Device Selection
Boot Manager

Transition System Load

OS Absent Application
UEFI Shell
Transient OS Boot Loader
Final OS Boot Loader

Run Time
OS environment
applications

The complete specification for UEFI is now 2098 pages of text available from the UEFI forum, and as such, is far more detailed than the limits of this paper. It's complete current source is at http://www.uefi.org/sites/default/files/resources/2_4_Errata_B.pdf. The transformation from CMOS/BIOS is significant and deserves some understanding and attention.

UEFI is an embrace and extend technology for the system bios. It does not eliminate fundamental firmware, but masks some of the complexity for developers and computer users. It also provides for a locked down mechanism for purchased systems such that their operating systems can not be removed or altered. It therefor provides a key objective of operating system vendors and computer system manufactures such that previously has been denied them by the open standards of BIOS and CMOS.

Upon powering up the system, BIOS bases systems have a very specific agenda of items that they must perform in order to be compliant with the specifications. With a BIOS the x86 CPU resets and loads a PC at the top of the one megabyte real mode address space which is where the BIOS program is resident. Then a jump instruction is set to move the PC to
an earlier location where the BIOS is run. The system can be reset from a cold boot or a warm boot. Flags determine which process to follow.
On a cold boot, the bios runs a "post". On a warm boot it does not.

Post identifies the systems parts and the CPU, RAM, interrupt and DMA controllers and other parts of the chipset, video display card, keyboard, hard disk drive, optical disc drive and other basic hardware. After posting, optional ROMs are searched for which extend functionality. These ROMs exist in upper memory, and the BIOS scans memory from 0x0C0000 to 0x0F0000 on the 2 KiB boundary. ROMs have a memory boundary of 0x55 0xAA followed by a byte that describes the number of 512 byte blocks that the expansion ROM sits at in real memory. A checksum is of the 512 byte block that is calculated and if valid, the execute jumps to the optional ROM which now controls the system. ROMS normally return back to the BIOS which scans for the next ROM until the entire sector of memory is scanned.

Finished with all this, the BIOS now calls INT 19h. INT 19H is a software interrupt that puts address 0019H onto the address bus and starts executing code found there. 0019H is normally a jump instruction. Usually this loads data from Head 0, Track 0 of Sector 1 of a disk. This would be the Master Boot Record (MBR). Information received by the Post determines which disks are attempted to locate a bootstrap loader, installing it into memory location 0x0000:0x7C00. The bloatstrap loader reads in the partition table and the operating system. [2]

The bios is a dumb device that does not process instructions from the boot sector. This is left to the bootstrap program. What is most important to understand is that the entire BIOS specification is very specific with exact definitions of interrupts, memory mappings, from interrupt definitions, hard drive specification and a plethora of exact locations and limitations in order to get from power of to OS running. Much of this detail was created because the x86 specification was designed for the purpose of emulating the specific IMB/PC XT product and architecture. The new UEFI specification buries much of this specification and leaves the implementation specifics to individual firmware companies. Under the hood, one motherboard under UEFI might use an entirely unique set of addressing schemes and interrupts then another, as long as BOTH end up showing an interface that complies with the UEFI specification.

"While BIOS is fundamentally a solid piece of firmware, UEFI is a programmable software interface that sits on top a computer's hardware and firmware (and indeed UEFI can and does sit on top of BIOS). Rather than all of the boot code being stored in the motherboard's BIOS, UEFI sits in the/EFI/ directory in some non-volatile memory; either in NAND on the motherboard, on your hard drive, or on a network share (more onthat later)." [3]

Bootloaders have been constrained to fit in 446 bits of the master bootrecord and run in 32k of system memory. These are called first stage boot loaders and the partition tables are in a default 64 byte partition table with four primary partitions, in its most generic form. Boatloaders most often load secondary boot loaders that are more flexible, such and GRUB. These loaders allow for multiple operating system installation or to load operating systems in different states. They read partition tables and load systems accordingly.

UEFI takes a different approach. As one tech blogger wrote, "Now let's look at how booting works on a UEFI system. Even if you don't grasp the details of this post, grasp this: it is completely different. Completely and utterly different from how BIOS booting works. You cannot apply anyof your understanding of BIOS booting to native UEFI booting. You cannot make a little tweak to a system designed for the world of BIOS booting and apply it to native UEFI booting. You need to understand that it is a completely different world." [4] I think this is overstated. Eventually every computer system has to do exactly what a BIOS based system does. It has to reach into the architecture of a computer, identify some subset of its working parts, and bootstrap a fully functional operating system into its memory while running the operating systems viable instruction set. UEFI is an attempt to hide much of this hardware complexity and substitute it with software complexity that looks simpler. There are inherent problems with this approach, the first being is the scale of the introduced complexity. Let's review some of this introduced complexity.

One of the first changes to the booting process involved the change from the MBR standard to what is no known as GPART or GPT standard. There was an essential problem to the original BIOS specification that was simply outgrown over time, namely the limitation of the size of partitions that could be read from hard drives. The Master Boot Record, is that special sector at the very beginning of a fixed disk that describes the partition table of the disk and contains the primary boot loader. The MBR is limited to 32 bits for addressing partitions and with a sector size set at 512 bytes, hard drive addressing is limited to a shade over 2 terabytes in size. In order address partitions greater than 2 terabytes, another scheme was needed. That scheme came the way of the GUID Patition Table,
(GPT).

This is the layout for a modern Master Boot Record:

ADDRESS	Description	Size in Bytes
Hex Dec		

+000h +0 Bootstrap code area (part 1) 218

+0DAh +218 0000h Disk timestamp[4][b]
(optional, MS-DOS 7.1-8.0
(Windows 95B/98/98SE/ME),
alternatively can serve as OEM
loader signature with NEWLDR) 2
+0DCh +220 original physical drive (80h-FFh) 1
+0DDh +221 seconds (0-59) 1
+0DEh +222 minutes (0-59) 1
+0DFh +223 hours (0-23) 1
+0E0h +224 Bootstrap code area (part 2, code
entry at +000h) 216 (or 222)
+1B8h +440 32-bit disk signature
Disk signature (optional, UEFI,
Windows NT/2000/Vista/7 and other
OSes) 4
+1BCh +444 0000h
(5A5Ah if copy-protected)   2
+1BEh +446 Partition entry #1
Partition table
(for primary partitions) 16
+1CEh +462 Partition entry #2 16
+1DEh +478 Partition entry #3 16
+1EEh +494 Partition entry #4 16
+1FEh +510 55h Boot signature[a] 2
+1FFh +511 AAh

Total size: 218 + 6 + 216 + 6 + 4×16 + 2 512 (from WIKIPEDIA)

GUID Partition Tables, which are now a key component of the UEFI specification, feature divisions of memory through the modern LBA placement and memory scheme. Previously, hard drive locations were identified by the (Cylinder, Head, Sector) tuples, which identified a location through the raw location of the hard drive. As drives changes and new media emerged, CHS was replaced by LBA (Logical Block Addressing).[5] The protective MBR would be in LBA0. The GPT header is in LBA1 which has a pointer to the Partition Table or a Partition Entry Array. [6] The Partition Array, by UEFI standards must have a minimum 16,384 bytes which allows for addressing space to 18 Exabyte with up to128 partitions. The GPT has a partition header that defines the tables characteristics. It lives always in LBA1. GUID is a system for uniquely identifying computing components as defined in the UUID Standard. It is 32 Hex couples, 128 bit values.

The UEFI standard includes a native executable tongue called the EFI Byte Code (EBC if you are keeping track). This is a 'virtual' machine in which the firmware can be written to and for which implementation will happen on any hardware architecture, regardless of the CPU. In C programming, it requires the use of efi and efilib headers and a complex linkage to cross compile to the efi binary code. A GNU-EFI package exists and a sample program for a native EFI firmware binary is demonstrated by Roderick W. Smith at http://www.rodsbooks.com/efi-programming/hello.html. His sample program includes as follows:

```
#include <efi.h>
```

```c
#include <efilib.h>

EFI_STATUS
EFIAPI
efi_main (EFI_HANDLE ImageHandle, EFI_SYSTEM_TABLE *SystemTable) {
    InitializeLib(ImageHandle, SystemTable);
    Print(L"Hello, world!\n");

    return EFI_SUCCESS;
}
```

Notice how main is replaces with efi_main

The compilation would require a cross platform compile to EFI native binary and a complex makefile is provided by Mr Smith as follow:

```makefile
ARCH            = $(shell uname -m | sed s,i[3456789]86,ia32,)

OBJS            = main.o
TARGET          = hello.efi

EFIINC          = /usr/include/efi
EFIINCS         = -I$(EFIINC) -I$(EFIINC)/$(ARCH) -I$(EFIINC)/protocol
LIB             = /usr/lib64
EFILIB          = /usr/lib64/gnuefi
EFI_CRT_OBJS    = $(EFILIB)/crt0-efi-$(ARCH).o
EFI_LDS         = $(EFILIB)/elf_$(ARCH)_efi.lds

CFLAGS          = $(EFIINCS) -fno-stack-protector -fpic \
  -fshort-wchar -mno-red-zone -Wall
ifeq ($(ARCH),x86_64)
  CFLAGS += -DEFI_FUNCTION_WRAPPER
endif

LDFLAGS         = -nostdlib -znocombreloc -T $(EFI_LDS) -shared \
  -Bsymbolic -L $(EFILIB) -L $(LIB) $(EFI_CRT_OBJS)

all: $(TARGET)

hello.so: $(OBJS)
ld $(LDFLAGS) $(OBJS) -o $@ -lefi -lgnuefi

%.efi: %.so
objcopy -j .text -j .sdata -j .data -j .dynamic \
-j .dynsym  -j .rel -j .rela -j .reloc \
--target=efi-app-$(ARCH) $^ $@
```

Note that Makefiles are tab sensitive so you will need to assure the format of this file accordingly.[7]

The UEFI standard includes the possible use of a shell. With the use of this shell, you can run arbitrary code. This is the Preboot environment of UEFI. In fact, Smith makes clear that this preboot environment can be useful for application development in several areas, reinforcing the idea that UEFI is very much operating system like in it's specification.

Wolfgang-Rosenbergsr, from Intel, has extensively documented a UEFI Shell and the EFI OpenShell available from http:www.tianocore.org. Among the items that the UEFI shell allows for is the execution of preboot programs, setup, operating system installation, testing of hardware and software, disk utilities, driver diagnostics, configuration modifications, moving files around and between the hard disk, floppy disk, CD-ROM, USB flash devices, and so on, to load a preboot EFI driver in the system (has an .efi suffix) such as network stacks, tcpip drivers, to, update old drivers in flash memory, load new drivers for plugin cards, and more.[8] This shell has two versions, Shell.efi and Shell_full.efi. Shell.efi fits on most current flash memories.

efi binary files start with the symbol efi_main that has two parameters, EFI_HANDLE ImageHandle and EFI_SYSTEM_TABLE *SystemTable. The system table is a C-style structure with the following entries:

```c
typedef struct _EFI_SYSTEM_TABLE {
    EFI_TABLE_HEADER                    Hdr;

    CHAR16                              *FirmwareVendor;
    UINT32                              FirmwareRevision;

    EFI_HANDLE                          ConsoleInHandle;
    SIMPLE_INPUT_INTERFACE              *ConIn;

    EFI_HANDLE                          ConsoleOutHandle;
    SIMPLE_TEXT_OUTPUT_INTERFACE        *ConOut;

    EFI_HANDLE                          StandardErrorHandle;
    SIMPLE_TEXT_OUTPUT_INTERFACE        *StdErr;

    EFI_RUNTIME_SERVICES                *RuntimeServices;
    EFI_BOOT_SERVICES                   *BootServices;

    UINTN                               NumberOfTableEntries;
    EFI_CONFIGURATION_TABLE             *ConfigurationTable;

} EFI_SYSTEM_TABLE;
```

These listed handles, likewise have application interfaces that directly tie to firmware defined modules. For example, one can call ConOut->OutputString() to print to the console. Firmware is required to make available a set of binary compatible libraries for extensive program building. EFI_RUNTIME_SERVICES accesses a firmware services which are available in the preboot environment and when the Operating System takes control of the system. These services include system clock functions, NVRAM variables, and system reset operations. This is unlike EFI_BOOT_SERVIES which are only available during the preboot phase. 7

In order to accommodate all this complex preboot operating system, UEFI specifies that boot medium must have an EFI partition which contains binaries, and bootloader. This is something that must astute observers have seen on flash drives for a number of years. In order to allow them to function as bootable devices, they have EFI partitions on their front. These small partitions must be either FAT12, FAT16 or FAT32. All UEFI compliant systems must be able to read all of these FAT variations.

"The file system supported by the Extensible Firmware Interface is based on the FAT file system. EFI defines a specific version of FAT that is explicitly documented and testable. Conformance to the EFI specification and its associate reference documents is the only definition of FAT that needs to be implemented to support EFI. To differentiate the EFI file system from pure FAT, a new partition file system type has been defined." 4

As such a EFI partition is a partition defined as such type in a gpart record and which has a valid EFI approved version of the FAT file system
installed within it.

UEFI specifies a UEFI Boot Manager. Since the purpose of all this is to boot an operating system, something the BIOS Specification seems to do so matter of factly, UEFI includes a boot manager with specifications WITHIN its environment, rather than leaving it to the operating system. Just as BIOS reads extensions that it expects to find at predefined locations, the UEFI Boot Manager is defined as follows:

> "The UEFI boot manager is a firmware policy engine that can be configured by
> modifying architecturally defined global NVRAM variables. The boot manager will attempt to load
> UEFI drivers and UEFI applications (including UEFI OS boot loaders) in an order defined by
> the global NVRAM variables." 4

For those used to looking at the CMOS over the years, this is largely the "rubber hits the road" change to the booting process with UEFI. The configuration system is entirely different and it is not alway clear what you are looking at when your not experienced with UEFI when trying to install an operating system. UEFI can be configured. You can alter your boot menu when you start your system and activate the boot manager. You can add drives, and twist up firmware configurations, even over clock the CPU. Because of the size of the EFI Partition, this application can be a graphic user interface, or a cursors like configuration menu. Linux comes with a tool to help work with your boot manager called efibootmgr.[9] It produces output such as this, when run from user space:

```
[root@system directory]# efibootmgr -v
BootCurrent: 0002
Timeout: 3 seconds
BootOrder: 0003,0002,0000,0004
Boot0000* CD/DVD Drive  BIOS(3,0,00)
Boot0001* Hard Drive    HD(2,0,00)
Boot0002* Fedora        HD(1,800,61800,6d98f360-cb3e-4727-8fed-
5ce0c040365d)File(\EFI\fedora\grubx64.efi)
Boot0003* opensuse      HD(1,800,61800,6d98f360-cb3e-4727-8fed-
5ce0c040365d)File(\EFI\opensuse\grubx64.efi)
```

```
Boot0004* Hard Drive     BIOS(2,0,00)P0: ST1500DM003-9YN16G        .
[root@system directory]#
```

Here you can see the option: BootOrder which is to load first opensuse (with its load path within the EFI partition specified), and then Fedora and then the CD/DVD, and finally Hard Drive under BIOS(2,0,00)

Notice the EFI Paths described in the output of efibootmanager. They can point at any device object that the firmware presents. This is not just Hard Drives, but network devices, USB ports or devices not yet invented. These paths are defined in the specification under EFI_DEVICE_PATH_PROTOCOL. These protocols are very difficult to learn and understand. They are defined in language programing, initially by Intel and later by other vendors. An example is given by Intel in slide 13 and 14 in their presentation on UEFI located at http://www.feishare.com/attachments/105_202%20UEFI-Drivers.pdf and where it states:

```
Device Path Protocol - Example
GUID

#define EFI_DEVICE_

PATH_PROTOCOL_GUID \
{0x09576e91,0x6d3f,0x11d2,0x8e,0x39,0x00,0xa0,0xc9,0x69,0x72, 0x3b}

Protocol Interface Structure

typedef struct _EFI_DEVICE_PATH_PROTOCOL {
   UINT8 Type;
   UINT8 SubType;
   UINT8 Length[2];
} EFI_DEVICE_PATH_PROTOCOL;

• The device path describes the location of the device
the handle is for
• A UEFI driver may access only a physical device for
which it provides functionality.
```

The slides go on to give an example of a SCSI Bus interface and a discussion of the language implementation.

Phoenix company defines the fully paths for devices as follows. In this exampe the path names are spelled out for the subset of devices that Phoneix at least is supporting with this long and verbose specification for device paths and structure within their firmware.[10] I quote the exact specification in order to underscore how complex path naming is which underlines that UEFI does not, as it claims, remove complexity from the booting process. It does organize the complexity to make it more managable in some instances.

_____

_____

```
*GUID
```

```
#define EFI_DEVICE_PATH_PROTOCOL_GUID \
  {0x09576e91,0x6d3f,0x11d2,0x8e,0x39,0x00,0xa0,0xc9,0x69,0x72,0x3b}

*Protocol Interface Structure

#include EFI_PROTOCOL_CONSUMER(DevicePath) // for protocol
#include "Efi\EfiDevicePath.h"            // for #define & structures

extern EFI_GUID gEfiDevicePathProtocolGuid;

typedef struct _EFI_DEVICE_PATH_PROTOCOL {
  UINT8 Type;
  UINT8 SubType;
  UINT8 Length[2];
} EFI_DEVICE_PATH_PROTOCOL;

Members
Member Description
Type The type of device path node.

#define HARDWARE_DEVICE_PATH          0x01
#define ACPI_DEVICE_PATH              0x02
#define MESSAGING_DEVICE_PATH         0x03
#define MEDIA_DEVICE_PATH             0x04
#define BBS_DEVICE_PATH               0x05
#define END_DEVICE_PATH_TYPE          0x7f

SubType The sub-type of the device path now. The meaning depends on Type.
For HARDWARE_DEVICE_PATH:

#define   HW_PCI_DP                   0x01
#define   HW_PCCARD_DP                0x02
#define   HW_MEMMAP_DP                0x03
#define   HW_VENDOR_DP                0x04
#define   HW_CONTROLLER_DP            0x05

For ACPI_DEVICE_PATH:

#define   ACPI_DP                     0x01
#define   ACPI_EXTENDED_DP            0x02
#define   ACPI_ADR_DP                 0x03

For MESSAGING_DEVICE_PATH:

#define   MSG_ATAPI_DP                0x01
#define   MSG_SCSI_DP                 0x02
#define   MSG_FIBRECHANNEL_DP         0x03
```

```
#define   MSG_1394_DP                  0x04
#define   MSG_USB_DP                   0x05
#define   MSG_I2O_DP                   0x06
#define   MSG_INFINIBAND_DP            0x09
#define   MSG_VENDOR_DP                0x0a
#define   MSG_MAC_ADDR_DP              0x0b
#define   MSG_IPv4_DP                  0x0c
#define   MSG_IPv6_DP                  0x0d
#define   MSG_UART_DP                  0x0e
#define   MSG_USB_CLASS_DP             0x0f
#define   MSG_USB_WWID_DP              0x10
#define   MSG_DEVICE_LOGICAL_UNIT_DP 0x11
#define   MSG_SATA_DP                  0x12
#define   MSG_ISCSI_DP                 0x13
```

For MEDIA_DEVICE_PATH:

```
#define   MEDIA_HARDDRIVE_DP           0x01
#define   MEDIA_CDROM_DP               0x02
#define   MEDIA_VENDOR_DP              0x03
#define   MEDIA_FILEPATH_DP            0x04
#define   MEDIA_PROTOCOL_DP            0x05
```

For BBS_DEVICE_PATH:

```
#define   BBS_BBS_DP                   0x01
```

For END_DEVICE_PATH_TYPE:

```
#define END_ENTIRE_DEVICE_PATH_SUBTYPE    0xFF
#define END_INSTANCE_DEVICE_PATH_SUBTYPE 0x01
```

Length The entire length of this device path node, including this header, in bytes.

Description
The executing IEFI Image may use the device path to match its own device drivers to the particular device.
Note that the executing UEFI OS loaderand UEFI application images must access all physical devices via
Boot Services device handles until ExitBootServices() is successfully called.

A UEFI driver may access only a physical device for which it provides functionality.

```
TypeSubTypeStructure
```

```
HARDWARE_DEVICE_PATHHW_PCI_DPPCI_DEVICE_PATH
HW_PCCARD_DPPCCARD_DEVICE_PATH
HW_MEMMAP_DPMEMMAP_DEVICE_PATH
```

HW_VENDOR_DPVENDOR_DEVICE_PATH
HW_CONTROLLER_DP CONTROLLER_DEVICE_PATH
ACPI_DEVICE_PATHACPI_DPACPI_HID_DEVICE_PATH
ACPI_EXTENDED_DP
ACPI_EXTENDED_HID_DEVICE_PATH ACPI_ADR_DP
ACPI_ADR_DEVICE_PATH
MESSAGING_DEVICE_PATHMSG_ATAPI_DPATAPI_DEVICE_PATH
MSG_SCSI_DPSCSI_DEVICE_PATH
MSG_FIBRECHANNEL_DP
FIBRECHANNEL_DEVICE_PATH
MSG_1394_DPF1393_DEVICE_PATH
MSG_USB_DPUSB_DEVICE_PATH
MSG_USB_CLASS_DP USB_CLASS_DEVICE_PATH
MSG_USB_WWID_DP USB_WWID_DEVICE_PATH
MSG_DEVICE_LOGICAL_UNIT_DP
DEVICE_LOGICAL_UNIT_DEVICE_PATH
MSG_I2O_DEPI2O_DEVICE_PATH
MSG_MAC_ADDR_DP MAC_ADDR_DEVICE_PATH
MSG_IPv4_DPIPv4_DEVICE_PATH
MSG_IPv6_DPIPv6_DEVICE_PATH
MSG_INFINIBAND_DP INFINIBAND_DEVICE_PATH
MSG_UART_DPUART_DEVICE_PATH
MSG_VENDOR_DPVENDOR_DEVICE_PATH

MSG_VENDOR_DP,GUID =
DEVICE_PATH_MESSAGING_PC_ANSI ---

MSG_VENDOR_DP,
GUID = DEVICE_PATH_MESSAGING_PC_VT_100

MSG_VENDOR_DP, GUID =
DEVICE_PATH_MESSAGING_PC_VT_100_PLUS

MSG_VENDOR_DP, GUID =
DEVICE_PATH_MESSAGING_PC_UTF8

MSG_VENDOR_DP, GUID =
DEVICE_PATH_MESSAGING_FLOW_CONTROL
UART_FLOW_CONTROL_DEVICE_PATH

MSG_VENDOR_DP, GUID =
DEVICE_PATH_MESSAGING_SAS
SAS_DEVICE_PATH MSG_ISCSI_DP
ISCSI_DEVICE_PATH MSG_SATA_DP
SATA_DEVICE_PATH

MEDIA_DEVICE_PATHMEDIA_HARDDRIVE_DP

```
HARDDRIVE_DEVICE_PATHMEDIA_CDROM_DPCDROM_DEVICE_PATH
MEDIA_VENDOR_DPVENDOR_DEVICE_PATH
MEDIA_VENDOR_DP, GUID= UNKNOWN_DEVICE_GUID
UNKNOWN_DEVICE_VENDOR_DEVICE_PATH
MEDIA_FILEPATH_DP
FILEPATH_DEVICE_PATH MEDIA_PROTOCOL_DP
MEDIA_PROTOCOL_DEVICE_PATH
BBS_DEVICE_PATHBBS_BBS_DPBBS_BBS_DEVICE_PATH
```

In section 8.3 of the original Intel Specification, EFI Specification version 1.10, dated December 1, 2002, six paths are defined as follows:

Device Path Nodes
There are six major types of Device Path nodes:

1) Hardware Device Path. This Device Path defines how a device is attached to the resource domain of a system, where resource domain is simply the shared memory, memory mapped I/O, and I/O space of the system.

2) ACPI Device Path. This Device Path is used to describe devices whose enumeration is not described in an industry-standard fashion. These devices must be described using ACPI AML in the ACPI name space; this Device Path is a linkage to the ACPI name space.

3) Messaging Device Path. This Device Path is used to describe the connection of devices outside the resource domain of the system. This Device Path can describe physical messaging information (e.g., a SCSI ID) or abstract information (e.g., networking protocol IP addresses).

4) Media Device Path. This Device Path is used to describe the portion of a medium that is being abstracted by a boot service. For example, a Media Device Path could define which partition on a hard drive was being used.

5) BIOS Boot Specification Device Path. This Device Path is used to point to boot legacy operating systems; it is based on the BIOS Boot Specification Version 1.01. Refer to the References appendix for details on obtaining this specification.

6) End of Hardware Device Path. Depending on the Sub-Type, this Device Path node is used to indicate the end of the Device Path instance or Device Path structure.[11]

You can see this specification reflected in the Phoenix development protocols. Overall, there is a very verbose and user unfreindly naming convention for identifying bootable objects within the UEFI bootloader, all of which can be quite frightful when a user is confronted with deleting a driver that the firmware initially places on the boot menu. Firmware writers need to be careful to include a return to default configuration in order to save the end user from themselves.

Returning back to the output of our sample efibootmgr output, and after reviewing some of the specifications of EFI_DEVIDE_PATH_PROTOCOL, we can now disect some of this output with better edification:

```
[root@system directory]# efibootmgr -v
BootCurrent: 0002
Timeout: 3 seconds
BootOrder: 0003,0002,0000,0004
Boot0000* CD/DVD Drive   BIOS(3,0,00)
Boot0001* Hard Drive     HD(2,0,00)
Boot0002* Fedora
HD(1,800,61800,6d98f360-cb3e-4727-8fed-
5ce0c040365d)File(\EFI\fedora\grubx64.efi)
Boot0003* opensuse
HD(1,800,61800,6d98f360-cb3e-4727-8fed-
5ce0c040365d)File(\EFI\opensuse\grubx64.efi)
Boot0004* Hard Drive     BIOS(2,0,00)P0: ST1500DM003-9YN16G        .
```

Boot0000, and Boot0004 are evidently legacy bios boot entries. Boot0002 and Boot0003 are native UEFI entries which point to different secondary boot loaders, both being on the same hard drive device and both executables residing in the EFI active partition, one for fedora and one for opensuse. Boot0001 is a UEFI default boot if all else fails. This is similar to a bios boot but the UEFI boot loader looks on the specified hard drive for a efi binary based on the system architecture, such as \EFI\BOOT\BOOTx64.EFI (for a x86 64 bit arch).

An important and controversial component of the UEFI specification is the secure boot configuration. Theoretically the secure boot is designed to address a security issue, which is a root kit attack. In real life, this is a non-issue and of no concern whatsoever. What the secure boot mechanism is actually for is to protect the vendors who wrote this specification from the installation of competitive products on hardware which they have OEM contracts with. Root kits require physical access to sensitive parts of a computer system. Without physical security, one can never have security of any kind. As a vector, firmware root kits are one of the hardest attacks on a digital system. Gartner reports that in 2013 over 19 BILLION dollars was spent on security software, nearly all of it targeted for Microsoft Windows viruses and worms.[12] The 2013 security report from Sohpos outlines nearly ever possible vector for malware on all platforms, with special emphasis on emerging devices. In their comprehensive report firmware attacks are not considered even a viable vector.[13] The standing threat is still standard Microsoft Windows. For example, Microsoft shipped its latest operating system with a sliding gadget that immediately had to be withdrawn because it served as a vector for multiple malware attacks. [14]

"Applying the automated Microsoft Fix it solution described in
Microsoft Knowledge Base Article 2719662 disables the Windows
Sidebar experience and all Gadget functionality.

Recommendation. Customers who are concerned about vulnerable
or malicious Gadgets should apply the automated Microsoft Fix
it solution as soon as possible. For more information, see the
Suggested Actions section of this advisory." [15]

So what is the problem being addressed? First and foremost, Secure Boot is about vendor control and not security. This is obvious. No true expert on cryptography or security has been able to demonstrate that removal of security and keys from the users improves security of a system. And furthermore there is scant evidence of a security issue within the prebooting environment, that is up until now. In fact, Richard Wilkins, of Phoenix Technologies, and Brian Richardson Intel Corporation, write in their September 2013 paper on UEFI and computer security 3 pages of outlined possible security issues and maleware efforts, including documented in the wild programs and research test programs and show current threats outside of the theoretical.

To quote one blogger at zdnet:

> "You should do your readership a huge favor. Interview a world-class
> cryptography expert [I suggest Ron Rivest over at M.I.T., the "R" in RSA as
> you know], and ask him/her the following question:
>
> 1. "Is there any technical reason whatsoever that UEFI-Secure Boot
> should be tied to any particular OS vendor in order for the end-user to
> realize the benefit of secure-boot?"
> 2. "How would you have implemented secure-boot?"
>
> Ask him/her to go into as much detail as reasonable, so that all the tech-
> heads who read your journal are able to follow along and conclude for
> themselves that the binding to Windows is entirely artificial and
> concocted by Microsoft.
>
> The reason for doing such an interview is very important: There are a
> lot of people, including the U.S. Department of Justice, for whom
> cryptography is a kind of black magic. They do not know what is fact and
> what is fiction, even after reading the specifications for asymmetric
> crypto, because it takes a while to be able to understand crypto primitives
> well-enough to know that nobody is pulling the wool over your eyes. "

In fact, it seems very apparent that the perceived threat to system security, such as any exist at the preboot level, is largely from the UEFI environment itself. It actually boots an mini-operating system and the EFI Partition can represent a whole new security hole, especially when linked to a non-secure operating system such as Microsoft Windows.

"The examples outlined above describe similar attack methods. The bootkit is deployed in the form of a UEFI executable , to masquerade as the default operating system boot loader. The bootkit then launches a patched version of the operating system loader, adding exploit code before the operating system loads malware protection...While rootkits and bootkits are an issue for any system, including legacy BIOS environments, they present a unique challenge to the UEFI ecosystem. The entire philosophy behind UEFI is to standardize and allow for extensibility of the pre - boot interface. While this openness and standardization can make the system vulnerable to attacks that would have been more difficult in legacy BIOS , it is important to acknowledge that legacy BIOS had very limited provisions for detection or defense. Any optimal solution for UEFI needs to embrace flexibility , while limiting attack vectors, mitigating risk, promoting possibilities and providing methods for manufacturers and users to control their security policy."[17]

This heady combination of desire for vendor control, an inherently insecure preboot environment, and consideration of the significant legal ramifications, there has been good reason for the Secure Boot protocols and their abuse by Microsoft Corporation, who in addition to wanting system control as a means of market dominance, also understands that they have an insecure operating system just ripe for being taken advantage of through the UEFI security hole which they will allow access to.

Secure Boot is a system within EFI where the binaries for the operating system and other binaries are cryptographically signed. This prevents tampering as the system will not boot a binary which is not signed when secure boot is turned on within the UEFI firmware.

What is a cryptographically signed binary? Most cryptography today uses asymmetrical (known also as public key) encryption. In its simplest form, someone creates a private key and safely stores it. An algorithm allows for the creation of a many public keys. A plain message can then use an algorithm to encrypt the plain message. The algorithm is such, however, where ONLY THE PRIVATE KEY can decrypt the encrypted message. There are many versions of asymmetric encryption standards including Diffie–Hellman key exchange protocol, DSS (Digital Signature Standard), which incorporates the Digital Signature Algorithm, ElGamal, Various elliptic curve techniques, Various password-authenticated key agreement techniques, Paillier cryptosystem, RSA encryption algorithm (PKCS#1), Cramer–Shoup cryptosystem, YAK authenticated key agreement protocol and others.[18]

Steps for Standard Encryption of a message using Public Keys:

```
Step 1: LONG_DATA_STREAM ==> Encryption ==> Private Key
Step 2: Private Key ==> Asymmetric Algorithm ==> Public Key (make as many
as you
want)
Step 3: Distribute Public Key
Step 4: Plain Message ==> Encrypt with Public Key ==> Unreadable Message
Step 5: Unreadable Message can only be decrypted with the PRIVATE key **
Step 6: Unreadable Message ==> DECRYPT with Private Key ==> Plain Message
```

Signing some data with a binary signature is a bit more complex. It requires that with a public key, one can determine that a message was signed with the public keys private key, although it can not decrypt the message. In the case of signatures, it is not necessary to decrypt the signature, in fact the message is gibberish in content, but only that it was generated from a specific private key. RSA is an algorithm that can perform this task and the entry in Wikipedia explains binary signatures better than I could reformulate the process.

Suppose Alice uses Bob's public key to send him an encrypted message. In the message, she can claim to be Alice but Bob has no way of verifying that the message was actually from Alice since anyone can use Bob's public key to send him encrypted messages. In order to verify the origin of a message, RSA can also be used to sign a message.

Suppose Alice wishes to send a signed message to Bob. She can use her own private key to do so. She produces a hash value of the message, raises it to the power of d (modulo n) (as she does when decrypting a message), and attaches it as a "signature" to the message. When Bob receives the signed message, he uses the same hash algorithm in conjunction with Alice's public key. He raises the signature to the power of e (modulo n) (as he does when encrypting a message), and compares the resulting hash value with the message's actual hash value. If the two agree, he knows that the author of the message was in possession of Alice's private key, and that the message has not been tampered with since.

Since the hash value is constructed from the message itself, not only are we certain of the origins of the message (Alice), but also that the content has not been altered.[19] [20]

Secure Boot uses this technique to evaluate binaries that it boots. There are several levels of keys that the secure boot system uses, which creates a hierarchical system of trust. The 4 types of keys are as follows, from top to bottom:

PK - Platform Key, this is the top level public key on the system whose private key is owned by the OEM of the hardware. It is used to sign all other keys on the system.

KEK - Key Exchange Keys, is more properly described as a database of keys. These keys can only be entered into the firmware with PK key authority. The KEK has keys from the vendor, OEM, other operating system vendors, and the KEK entries authorize updates to the DB/DBX.

DB is the 'allowed' list of code that can execute, and for a Microsoft (R) Windows8 machine contains a Microsoft OS certificate, the Microsoft UEFI CA cert, and possibly other OSV/ISV entries

DBX is the 'disallowed and Blocked' list of code. 21,22

With a secure boot, the sequence of events for authorization to run binaries on the firmware is as follows:

The fireware loads binary objects and checks them against the DB and the DBX list. If the binary's signature is not within the DB list, or if it is in the DBX list, then it will not be run and the booting process will usually halt.

"As the boot process proceeds from an initial protected firmware core, it will load and execute additional sections of code, drivers and Option ROMs (code provided by peripheral manufacturers to enable their devices). Eventually this process culminates in the loading and execution of the operating system boot loader that starts the operating system execution. As each code section is loaded, and before it is executed, the firmware confirms that its signature matches one in its database of authorized signatures, and also that the signature is not in the forbidden database. This includes the operating system boot loader itself. What the firmware does with the signature matching information is a policy decision, and is not defined by the specification. Typically, unauthorized code will not be executed, and therefore, the system may not be able to complete the operating system bootstrap process." 22

The problem has been that Microsoft controls the signing agency for the KEK keys within the firmware. While the UEFI rules for a secure boot should allow for ownership control and the secure boot process, Microsoft has effectively blocked other signing agents from being brought on board by hardware manufacturers because of Microsoft's near monopoly and OEM sold x86 hardware. Initially it was a concern that x86 hardware would be blocked from installation of any non-Microsoft operating systems and binaries. Some of this concern has been alleviated by actions of Microsoft which assure that on x86 platforms that the terms of the Microsoft OEM will require that firmwares allow for the secure boot to be turned off. This is not true, however,for ARM processors, and Microsoft is not alone in locking down such devices.

There is a glitch in this solution, however. Going forward, it is a huge question as to if it is safe to run a UEFI booted system without a secure boot. The reason for this is exactly what was pointed out Wilkins and Richardson, which is that UEFI, with its virtual machine, readable partitions and userspace toolkits, makes a very target rich vector for malware in the future. 17 Just turning off secure boot on an industrial server comes with some serious risks that need to be accessed.

References:

_____

[1] http://www.tomshardware.com/reviews/intel-uefi-firmware,2486.html
[2] https://en.wikipedia.org/wiki/BIOS
[3] Sebastian Anthony on September 22, 2011
   http://wwwextremetech.com/computing/[96985]-demystifying-uefi-the-long-overdue-bios-replacement
[4] https://www.happyassassin.net/2014/01/25/uefi-boot-how-does-that-actually-work-then/
[5] Logical block addressing (LBA) is a common scheme used for specifying
the location of blocks of data stored on computer storage devices,
generally secondary storage systems such as hard disks
LBA is a particularly simple linear addressing scheme; blocks are located
by an integer index, with the first block being LBA [0], the second LBA 1,
and so on
[6] https://en.wikipedia.org/wiki/GUID_Partition_Table
[7] http://www.rodsbooks.com/efi-programming/hello.html
[8] https://software.intel.com/en-us/articles/uefi-shell/
[9] http://linux.die.net/man/8/efibootmgr
[10] http://wiki.phoenix.com/wiki/index.php/EFI_DEVICE_PATH_PROTOCOL
[11] EFI Specification 1.10 - December 1, 2002:
http://wwwintel.com/content/dam/doc/product-specification/efi-v[1]-10-specification.pdf
[12] http://www.gartner.com/newsroom/id/2762918
[13] http://www.sophos.com/en-us/medialibrary/PDFs/other/sophossecuritythreatreport2013.pdf
[14] https://nakedsecurity.sophos.com/2012/07/12/disable-windows-sidebar-gadgets/
[15] https://technet.microsoft.com/library/security/2719662
[16] http://www.zdnet.com/uefi-and-secure-boot-in-depth-7000012138/

Article titled "UEFI and secure boot in depth Summary: Q&A: My
questions on UEFI and secure boot, answered by Mark Doran, the president
of the UEFI Forum" by J.A. Watson March [13], 2013

[17]http://www.uefi.org/sites/default/files/resources/UEFI_Secure_Boot_in
_Modern_Computer_Security_Solutions_2013.pdf
[18] http://en.wikipedia.org/wiki/Public-key_cryptography
[19] http://en.wikipedia.org/wiki/RSA_%28cryptosystem%29#Signing_messages
[20]
http://upload.wikimedia.org/wikipedia/commons/2/2b/Digital_Signature_diag
ram.svg
[21] Victor Zimmer Engineering Blog September 28th, 2013
http://vzimmerblogspot.com/[2013]_09_01_archive.html
[22] Richard Wilkins, Ph.D., Brian Richardson: UEFI SECURE BOOT IN
MODERN COMPUTER SECURITY SOLUTIONS
http://wwwuefi.org/sites/default/files/resources/UEFI_Secure_Boot_in_Mode
rn_Computer_Security_Solutions_[2013].pdf

Ruben Safir ruben@mrbrklyn.com
See Bio Above

System On Chip
Integrated Circuits

Maneesh Kongara Feb 2015

An Integrated Circuit also known, as Monolithic Integrated Circuit is a set of electronic circuits embedded a single semiconductor material plate, usually silicon. The ICs usually are smaller than normal electric circuits, which are built with independent components. Despite their small size, ICs accommodate up to several billions of transistors and other electronic components in an area as small as a fingernail. With the advancement in technology, the width of each conducting lines in an IC is being made smaller and smaller, which now is a few tens of nanometers. ICs are experimental discoveries to prove that the semiconductor devices could replace the vacuum tubes in their functionality. Integrating a very large number of tiny transistors into a single chip was an enormous improvement over the previous manual assembly of circuits using discrete electronic components. The capability to produce in large quantities, reliability of the device and the building block approach of the ICs have ensured rapid adoption of ICs replacing the traditional design of using discrete transistors. Two major advantages of ICs over the discrete circuits are the cost and performance. The ICs are cheaper compared to the discrete circuits because the chips are printed as a single unit with all their components by photolithography rather than being constructed one transistor at a time like the discrete circuits. Moreover, it takes less material to build an IC than to build a discrete circuit. Compared to the discrete circuits, IC's switch components quickly and consume very little power because of the smaller size and smaller distance between the components. ICs are virtually used in all electronic devices today like the computers, mobile phones, and any other digital appliances. Evolution of Integrated Circuits

In the previous days, because of the lack of advancement in technology the integrated circuits were limited only to a very few transistors and low degree of integration keeping the design process relatively simple. With the progress in technology more and more transistors could be placed on a single chip, and improved designs, giving raise to new design principles.

The first ICs had a few tens of transistors, called "small scale integration". The small scale integration provided only a few logic gates because of the very few transistors being integrated. The term large scale integration was first used by Rolf Landauer, a scientist at IBM, describing a theoretical concept, from there came the terms for SSI, MSI, VLSI and ULSI.

The small scale integrated circuits played a very crucial role in early aerospace projects, which in turn helped to inspire development of the technology. The steep decline in the average price per IC dropped from $50.00 in 1962 to $2.33 in 1968 making IC to appear in consumer products by the end of 1960s.

The next development of ICs was in the late 1960s with the introduction of "medium scale integration" which contained a few hundreds of transistors on each chip. They were adapted widely because, while costing just a little more than the SSI, the MSI provided higher complexity using smaller circuit boards, less assembly work. Further development in ICs was with the introduction of "large scale integration" in the mid 1970s, with ICs consisting of tens of thousands of transistors per chip. Actual large scale integrated circuits, consisting of 10,000 transistors began to be produced around 1974 to be used for main memories of computers and the next generation of microprocessors.

The final step in the development of ICs was with the introduction of "large scale integration" in 1980s, which has progressed to "very large scale integration" in the present days. Initially the LSI had around hundreds of thousands of transistors, which continued beyond a few billions of transistors by the previous decade. The first one megabit RAM chips were introduced containing more than one million transistors in 1986. The microprocessors crossed the million mark line in 1989 and billion mark line in 2005. This trend continued to grow exponentially with introduction of chips containing tens of billions of memory transistor in 2007 and is still continuing to grow.

Moore's Law

"Moore's law" is the observation that, over the history of computing hardware, the number of transistors in a dense integrated circuit doubles approximately every two years (Wikipedia, 2014). Gordon E. Moore, co-founder of the Intel Corporation, proposed this law in 1965. His law is used in the semiconductor industries even today to guide long term planning and to set targets for future. The capabilities of largely used electronic devices today are very much influenced by Moore's law: quality adjustable microprocessor prices, capacity of the memory, sensors and also the size of pixels in cameras, are all progressing exponentially.

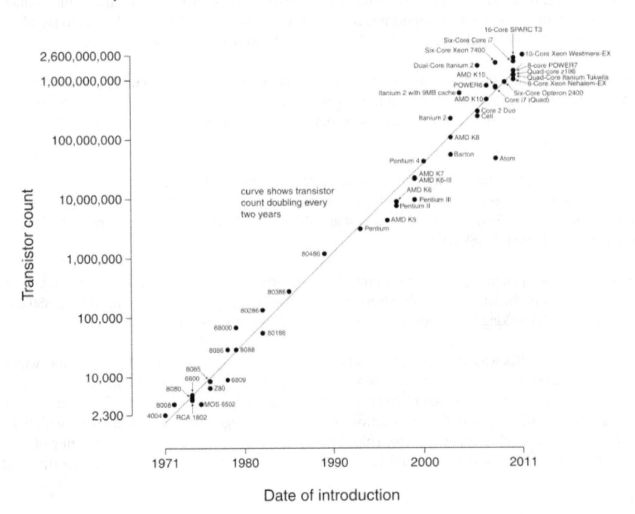

System on Chip

A system can be defined as a collection of all kinds of components or subsystems appropriately interconnected to perform the specified functions for end users. A system on chip is an integrated circuit that integrates all components of a computer or other electronic system into a single chip. It is possible for a system on chip to contain digital, analog, mixed signals and often radio frequency functions, all on a single chip substrate.

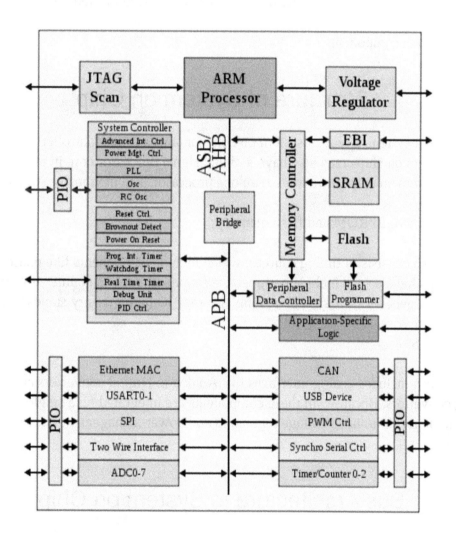

System on chip can also be defined as a high performance microprocessor, since we can program and instruct the microprocessor to perform a specific task. System on chip can also be defined as the efforts of integrating different types of silicon intellectual properties like the memory, microprocessor, logic gates and the circuitry on to a single chip.

Though microcontrollers are single chip systems, the major difference between microcontrollers and system on chip is that, microcontrollers have very little storage memory, typically under 100 KB, whereas system on

chip are generally used for high power processors which are capable of running Windows or Linux versions of software,
which need external memory and are used along with other peripheral devices.

System in package (SIP) is used as alternatives to system on chip when it is not feasible to construct a system on chip. System in package comprises of many chips in a single package. System on chip are more cost effective when produced in bulk compared to system in package because its packaging is simple and increases the yield of fabrication.

System on package is another alternative to system on chip when it is not possible to design a system on chip. System on package follows the concept of package on package stacking during the assembly of board. While system on chip contains various discrete electronic components interconnected on a single substrate, the system on package has
multiple layers of discrete components.

Structure of System on Chip

Just like an independent system, a typical system on chip contains a microcontroller and a microprocessor. Sometimes, a few system on chips may also have a digital signal processor core in place of a microprocessor, and multiprocessor system on chips have more than one processor. The next major component of a system on chip is memory blocks,
which include ROM, RAM, EPROM and flash memory.

The system on chip also consists of timing sources, which include components like phaselocked loops and oscillators. System on chip also can include peripheral components such as counter-timers, realtime timers, and power-on and reset generators. A system on chip also may include industry standard interfaces like universal serial bus, FireWire,
Ethernet, USART, and SPI.

The system on chip also includes analog interfaces like Analog to Digital convertors and may also contain Digital to Analog convertors. Because, all these components are integrated on a single chip together, it is essential for a system on chip to have voltage regulators and power management circuits to ensure safety of the system on chip.

Bus Architecture in System on Chip

All these components present on system on chip have to communicate with each other to facilitate proper functioning of the System on chip; this is facilitated by a bus structure. The bus structure can either be proprietary or industry-standard like the Advanced Microcontroller Bus Architecture (AMBA) by the ARM Holdings Industry. The role of Direct Memory Access controller or the DMA controller in the system on chip is to route data directly between external interfaces and the memory present on the chip bypassing the processor on the chip contributing to increased data throughput of the system on chip.

The advanced microcontroller bus architecture is an on-chip interconnect specification for connecting the various components of a system on chip and responsible for the communication among them for the proper functioning of the system on chip. The structure of the bus architecture on system on chip can be explained by the

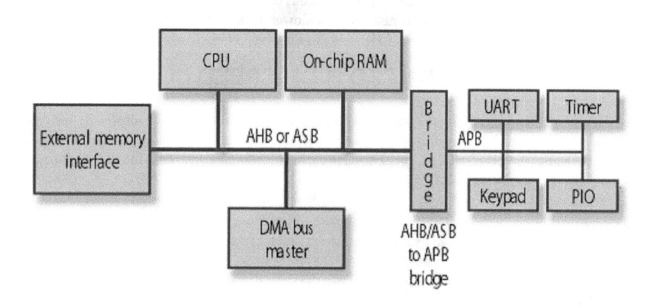

Fig: Bus organization of system on chip

AHB- Advanced High-Performance Bus

ASB- Advanced System Bus

APB- Advanced Peripheral Bus

following figure:

Advanced microcontroller bus architecture is implemented by a concept of multilevel bussing. AMBA generally involves a system bus and a low level peripheral bus. The system bus of AMBA generally includes either a advanced system bus (ASB) or a advanced high performance bus (AHB) and a advanced peripheral bus (APB).

Advanced microcontroller bus architecture (AMBA) was first implemented with the introduction of advanced system bus (ASB) in 1996. The second generation AMBA was the AMBA high-performance bus (AHB), introduced in the late 1990s, which implemented single clock-edge protocol. The third generation of AMBA 3 also known as the advances eXtensible interface (AXI) to implement high=performance interconnect and advanced tracing bus as the core sight on-chip debugging and tracing. The fourth generation of advanced microcontroller bus architecture was introduced in 2010 with the implementation of AMBA AXI4. The next generations followed by the introduction of AMBA 4 ACE in 2011 and AMBA 5 coherent hub interface in 2013 to reduce congestion in data transmission.

The advanced system bus or the ASB is used for cost effective and simple designs whereas the advanced high-performance bus or the AHB is implemented in sophisticated designs. These system buses are synchronous and non-multiplexed buses, which help in achieving data bursting and pipelining, and simple split transactions in more sophisticated implementation. These system busses are capable of supporting 32, 64 and 128 bit data implementation with a 32 bit address bus, as well as smaller byte and half word designs (Ray Weiss, 2001).

As it can be inferred from the above figure, the system buses are connected by a bridge as the master to the peripheral bus slave devices. The advanced peripheral bus or the APB serves as the peripheral bus, for a simple, low speed and low power implementation for slower devices, while the advanced high-performance bus AHB or the advanced highspeed bus AHB serve as the system bus.

ADVANCED HIGH-SPEED BUS:

The AHB is a multi-master with arbitrations and it takes the address on the bus followed by the data. The AHB supports wait-state intersection and has data-valid signal (HREADY). The AHB has separate read (HRDATA) and write (HWDATA) buses. The AHB, apart from supporting undefined length bursts and single transfers, also supports 4, 8, and
16 beat bursts.

All the bus operations are initiated by the bus masters, which can also serve as slaves. The master generated address is decoded by a central address decoder that provides a select signal to the addressed bus slave unit. The bus master can "lock" the bus, reserving it with the central arbiter for a series of locked transfer (Ray Weiss, 2001).

The slave unit can either terminate a transaction as an error, signal the master to retry or split the transaction for later completion. The split operation enables slave to differ the transaction until it is able to perform it, thereby, releasing the bus for other operations. When the slave signals a split it saves the master number (HMASTER\\[\\]). When the slave is ready to perform the transaction it signals the arbiter with the master number. The arbiter after receiving the master number, it restarts the transaction. A master cannot have more

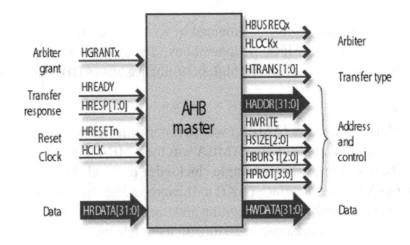

than one pending split at a time.

ADVANCED SYSTEM BUS:

The advanced system bus (AHB) is also a multi-master and pipelined bus and supports bursting. Compared to the AHB the ASB are simple busses, which do not support split functionality. The bus transfer types include non sequential and sequential Address Only. Address Only without data is used for idle cycles, bus master hand over cycles, and speculative address decoding. Where as nonsequential and sequential are implemented for single transfer and successive burst transfers respectively (Ray Weiss, 2001).

For every bus data transfer, the slave must respond, telling the master to continue (WAIT), that the transfer is done (DONE), that the transfer has resulted in an error condition (ERROR), that the slave can't accept any more transfers (LAST), or that the transfer should be retried (RETRACT). The WAIT, DONE, ERROR, LAST, and RETRACT signals are generated on the next cycle by the slave bus unit (Ray Weiss, 2001).

ASB is a non-multiplexed bus with a single data bus (BD\\[\\]). The BWRITE signal indicates the transfer direction (read or write), and BSIZE\\[\\] specifies the transfer size (width). The slaves don't have to check the bus addresses to see if they're being addressed. Instead, the bus address is used to generate a select signal

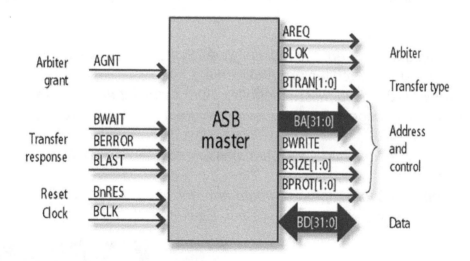

(DSELx) to select the addressed slave bus unit (Ray Weiss, 2001).

ADVANCED PERIPHERAL BUS:

Designed to support lowspeed peripherals such as UARTs, keypads, and PIO, the APB is a simple peripheral bus. All bus devices are slaves to the master, the bridge to the AHB, or ASB system bus. This is a static bus that provides a simple address, with latched address and control signals for easy interfacing. ARM recommends a dual Read and Write bus implementation, but APB can be implemented with a single tristated data bus (Ray Weiss, 2001).

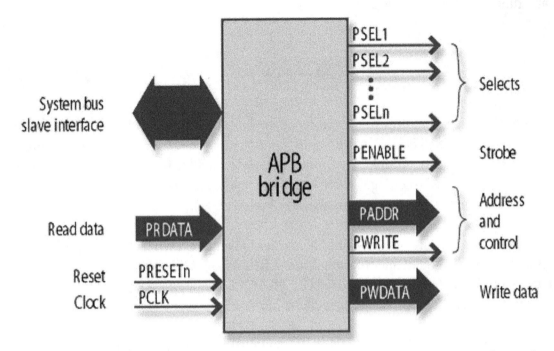

As a simple bus, the APB doesn't support bursting. Each transaction consists of 2 cycles: an address cycle (Setup state) and a data cycle (Enable state). The bus uses a single clock, PCLK. In Setup, the bus brings PSEL and PWRITE up, putting the address on the PADDR address bus. In the Enable state, it brings PENABLE up and places data on the PWDATA/PRDATA bus. The enable signal, PENABLE, is deasserted on next cycle.

References
1. System on chip, Wikipedia. http://en.wikipedia.org/wiki/System_on_a_chip
2. Advanced Microcontroller Bus Architecture, Wikipedia.
http://en.wikipedia.org/wiki/Advanced_Microcontroller_Bus_Architecture
3. AMBA Specifications home page. http://www.arm.com/products/system-ip/amba/amba-open-specifications.php
4. CoreLink system IP and Design. http://www.arm.com/products/system-ip/amba/index.php
5. AMBA Specifications.
http://infocenter.arm.com/help/index.jsp?topic=/com.arm.doc.ihi0011a/index.html
6. Advanced microprocessor bus architecture system. Electronic Design. Ray Weiss, 2001.

Maneesh Kongara
Graduate and Research Assistant
Long Island University
Masters Degree Candidate 2016
Computer Sciences, LIU
Brooklyn

```c
/*
 * ============================================================================
 *
 *       Filename:  binary_calc.c
 *
 *    Description:  Take two arguments, a decimal number and a base pair
 *    and return a representation of the number in the new base pair.
 *
 *        Version:  1.0
 *        Created:  09/17/2014 06:00:52 AM
 *       Revision:  none
 *       Compiler:  gcc
 *
 *         Author:  Ruben Safir (), ruben@mrbrklyn.com
 *        Company:  NYLXS
 *
 * ============================================================================
 */
#include <stdio.h>
#include <string.h>
#include <stdlib.h>


char * integer(char *, size_t, int);
char * decimal(char *, size_t, int);
char resultant [64];
char resultant2 [64];
int base, neg_flag=0;
char * tmp, * tmp2;


int main(int argc, char * argv[]){
        if(argc != 3){
                tmp = strtok(argv[0],"/");
                while ( (tmp2 = strtok(NULL,"/")) ){
                        tmp = tmp2;
                }
                fprintf (stderr, "usage: %s: Two Arguments \n \
                        ==> deminal integer\n\
                        ==>base\n\
                        The decimal is converted to the base number equivalent\n", tmp);
                return 1;
        }
        base = atoi(argv[2]);



        if(argv[1][0] == '.'){
                tmp = "0";
                tmp = strtok(argv[1], "."); //interger
        }
```

```c
        else{
                tmp = strtok(argv[1], "."); //interger
                tmp2 = strtok(NULL,".");    // decimal
        }
        integer(tmp, strlen(tmp), base);
        fprintf(stderr, "Done with integer\n");
        fprintf(stderr, "tmp2 ==> %s\n", tmp2);
        if(tmp2 != NULL)
                decimal(tmp2, strlen(tmp2), base);

        fprintf(stderr, "\nDone with decimal\n");

        printf ("%s.%s in base %d ==> ", tmp,tmp2, base);
        printf("%s.%s\n", resultant, resultant2);

        return 0;
}


char * integer(char * num, size_t size, int base){
        fprintf(stderr, "inside integer::\nnum==>  %s, size==> %zu, base==> %d\n", num,size,base);
        int i = 0,j = 0;
        int holder;
        int process = atoi(num);//dangerous function - no error check
        char buffer[64];

        if(base>10){
                fprintf( stderr, "Base greatere than 10\n");
                exit(1);
        }

        if (process < 0){
                neg_flag = 1;
                process = abs(process);
        }

        fprintf(stderr, "Entering Loop: i =>  %d, process ==> %d, base==> %d\n***\n", i,process,base);

        for(i=0;  process != 0 || i > 63; i++){
                fprintf(stderr, "\ni==> %d ", i);
                fprintf(stderr, "process==> %d base ==>%d \n", process, base);
                holder=process % base;
                process = process/base;
                fprintf(stderr, "holder==>%d ", holder );
                snprintf(&buffer[i],3 , "%d",holder);
                fprintf(stderr, "resultant==> %s \n",buffer);
                fprintf(stderr, "i==> %d process==> %d NEXT:\n****\n", i, process);
        }
```

```c
        if(i > 63){
                fprintf(stderr, "size overflow\n");
                exit(1);
        }
        fprintf(stderr, "Loop is finished\n\n");
        fprintf(stderr, "resultant==> %s \n\n",buffer);
        //reverse it//
        for(i = (strlen(buffer) - 1 ); i >= 0; i--,j++){
//              fprintf(stderr, "i--> %d j--> %d\n", i,j);
                *(resultant + j) = *(buffer + i);
        }
        fprintf(stderr, "Corrected resultant==> %s \n\n",resultant);
        return resultant;
}
char * decimal(char * num, size_t size, int base){
    fprintf(stderr, "Inside Decimal:\nnum =>%s size=>%zu base==>%d\n", num, size, base);
    int process = atoi(num);
    int remainder;
//    char dig;
    int i, max_dig=20; //no more than 20 digits although the reusltant2 is 64 digits
    int max_num = 1;
    for(i=0;i<size;i++){
       max_num = max_num * 10;
    }
    for(i = 0; i<max_dig; i++){
        process = process * base;
        fprintf(stderr, "\nprior to checking condition:  \nprocess ==> %d\nman_num ==> %d", process, max_num);
        if(process < 0){
            fprintf(stderr, "\nOverflow error\n");
            exit(1);
        }
        if(process >= max_num){
                remainder = process /  max_num;
                snprintf(&resultant2[i],2,"%d",remainder);
                fprintf(stderr, "\nresultant2-->%s", resultant2);
                process = process % max_num;
                if(process == 0){
                    return resultant2;
                }
        }else{
                snprintf(&resultant2[i],2,"%d",0);
                fprintf(stderr, "\nresultant2-->%s", resultant2);

        }
    }
    return resultant2;

}
```